HEALING LOVE

HEALING LOVE

Ralph A. DiOrio
Drawings by Susan Gaber

COMPLETE AND UNABRIDGED

AN IMAGE BOOK

Doubleday

NEW YORK LONDON TORONTO SYDNEY AUCKLAND

Image Book edition published October 1988 by special
arrangement with Doubleday.

Hardcover edition published January 1987 by Doubleday.

An Image Book
Published by Doubleday, a division of
Bantam Doubleday Dell Publishing Group, Inc.,
666 Fifth Avenue, New York, New York 10103

Image, Doubleday and the portrayal of
a cross intersecting a circle
are trademarks of Doubleday, a division of
Bantam Doubleday Dell Publishing Group, Inc.

Library of Congress Cataloging-in-Publication

DiOrio, Ralph A., 1930–
Healing love.

1. Prayers.   2. Meditations.   I. Title.
BV245.D635   1987   242   86-11572
ISBN 0-385-24678-1 (pbk.)

CONTENTS

Preface   9

PRAYERS

  A New Dawn   13
  Morning Prayers   14
  My Daily Intercessory Prayer   17
  At the End of the Day   19
  Evening Prayers   20
  Mercy Prayer   23
  Prayer for Cleansing   24
  Before Confession   26
  After Confession   27
  Song of Praise   31
  In Loving Adoration   32
  To the Holy Spirit   33
  Send Your Holy Spirit   34
  For the Gifts of the Holy Spirit   35
  Pentecost Prayer   37
  Prayer to St. Michael the Archangel   38
  Christ the King   39
  For Pope John Paul II   40
  Prayer for the Pope, Bishops, and All Clergy   41
  Prayer for Vocations   42
  When Leaving a Church   45
  For a Happy Death   46
  For Those to Be Married   47
  Just as I Am   48
  Prayer of Surrender   48

A Youth's Prayer   49
From a Mother's Heart   51
Prayer for My Mother   52
At the Feet of the Man from Galilee   55
An Invitation from Jesus   56
For Reconciliation   57
Advent Prayer   58
Prayer Before Christmas   59
A Christmas Prayer (1)   60
A Christmas Prayer (2)   61
Prayer for Generosity   62
Doce Me, Domine (Adaptation)   63
A Lenten Prayer   67
Prayer Before a Crucifix   68
Easter Prayer   69
Parents' Prayer for Their Children   70
For One's Mother and Father   71
Families for Prayer   72
For the Nation, State, or City   74
For Those Who Serve in Public Office   74
Healing Forgiveness   77
Short Healing Prayer (Rebuking Sickness)   78
A Prayer When Tired   79
Your Will Be Done   80
Invocation   81
I Believe in Miracles   83
Emotions   84
Be Open   87
For Insight   88
Pride and Vanity   89
Prayer of Faith in Time of Suffering   91
For Understanding   93
Song of My Soul   94
Anima Christi (Adaptation)   95
For My Sins   96
Out of the Depths, I Cry to You, O Lord   99

Come, Lord   100
The Lord Has Pardoned   101
For the Gift of Presence   102
An Offering of Faith   103
Intercessory Prayers   104
General Intercession   106
Hymn to Mary   111
Asking Mary's Intercession   112
To Jesus Through Mary   113
To Mary, Help of the Sick   114
Prayer of Abandonment   115
Prayer of Intercession to the Mother of God   116
Prayer of a Young Man   117
Memorare   118
Prayer to the Trinity   121
For God's Continued Presence   123
When Depressed   124
God's Unfailing Love   125
For a Troubled World   126
Healing Prayer   127
Healing Prayer for Wholeness   128
For All Emotional or Physical Pain   130
Prayer of Deliverance from Visual Disturbances   135
For the Hospitalized   136
For Little Children   137
A Community Prayer   138
For Miracles and Blessings   140
The Living Christ   141
Prayers for Employment   142
To Sustain One in Work   143
Before the Tabernacle   144
Holy Hour   145
A Priest's Prayer   149
Hurting One, We Hurt All   150
A Doctor's Prayer   151
To "Abba"   152

When Falling Short   153
For Psychological Problems   154
For Our Deep-Seated Hurts   155
Healing Love   159

REFLECTIONS

Fearful of Rejection   163
You Are Important to God   164
For Disorders   166
Jesus Calms the Storms   168
God Is Near   170
On Love   175
God Is Our Strength   176
For Teenagers   177
On Aging   178
For Shut-Ins: Life Is Not Over!   180
Brokenness   182
Peace   184
Trust in God   185
For a Troubled Marriage   189
Reconsecrating Marriage   191
Affirming Your Spouse   193
For a Mother and Her Sick Child   195
Hearts in Desperation   197
Surrender to God   200
Conversion: Jesus Is Calling You   202
Power of the Cross   207
The Resurrection and You   208

CONCLUSION: Speak Lord, Your Servant Listens

Jesus Speaks to Us   213

PREFACE

When was the last time that you *really* spoke to God, really spoke to Him from the prayer book of your own heart? When was the last time you told God that you loved Him just because you loved Him? When was the last time that you prayed without asking for something? When was the last time you made a holy hour alone with God—just the two of you?

Everyone needs to steal away for a little while each day to be alone in meditation. It gets us off the treadmill of superficial living. It shuts out the noise and the grind of the world around us and lets us hear the voice that speaks out of Silence. Give time to God! Go into stillness, solitude. Give yourself to God in submission with the prayer gift of God's presence.

> *"Lord, to whom are we to turn, except to*
> *You? Lord, we are filled with sins,*
> *with mistakes, with weariness. Heal us,*
> *Lord Jesus. Touch us, have mercy on us,*
> *have mercy on us, have mercy on us."*

This book brings together inspirational thought and contemporary prayers. The prayers touch upon a variety of needs and concerns. For the most part, they are prayers that were prayed spontaneously—during retreats, at healing services, while on crusades and at the celebration of Mass. Clearly, they come from my heart and soul and through the special blessing God has given me. Some prayers have been drawn from my tapes, from my former radio talks, and also from my book *The Healing Power of Affirmation*.

I am hopeful that all who read and pray with this book will find a "special prayer" or "message" that they feel was written just for them.

Through these prayers and reflections may you find your spiritual life enriched and your life so blessed by God that your soul is just one step closer on our mutual journey to home and to Him. I bless ✝ you in His Holy Name.

RALPH A. DIORIO
January 1986

PRAYERS

"Again I tell you, if two of you join your voices on earth to pray for anything whatever, it shall be granted to you by my Father in Heaven. Where two or three are gathered in My name, there I too will be present in their midst."

A New Dawn

Thank You, Lord. Thank You for this day. Thank You for the gift of life, for the gift of supportive friendship, the gift of a husband, the gift of a wife, the gift of a child. Thank You for the sunshine, the rain, the clouds. Thank You, Lord, for the roses that come in bloom. Thank You, Lord, for giving me life. This is a new day. O Lord, I know You wait for me "Till." Oh yes, that is Your word to me, "till." Till You come to me, I'll come to You, Lord, in the early hours of this morning, and not only this day, but all the days of my life.

My Lord, this day, Your gift to me, I ask You to bless. I ask You, please, Lord, to think today through me. Speak, Lord, through me. Act, Dear Lord, through me with ease. No matter what, at work or play, live through me. Laugh through me. Love through me today. O my God, my will, my life, I give it to You. Show me, Lord, grow in me, Lord. Let me grow in You. Let me give the gift of You, through me, to the world. Quicken me anew, dear Lord. Thank You, Lord. Amen.

Morning Prayers

In the name of the Father and of the Son and of the Holy Spirit. Amen.

O Lord, open my lips,

and my mouth shall proclaim your praise.

Let us place ourselves in the presence of God. We firmly believe, O God,

That You are here present, that You see us, hear us, and know all our thoughts, all our desires, and even the most secret movements of our hearts, and that You are graciously willing to hear our prayers.

Let us adore Almighty God, and thank Him for all His blessings. We adore You, O God,

And acknowledge You to be our sovereign Lord and Master, upon whom we depend for all we are and all we possess. We thank You for creating us in Your image and likeness, for redeeming us by the precious blood of Your Son, Jesus Christ. We thank You, also, for preserving us during the night, and, in general, for all the graces which we have constantly received from the first moment of our existence.

Let us beg of God grace to spend this day well, and let us offer to Him all our actions. O Almighty God,

Who brought us safely to the beginning of this day, save us by Your grace from falling into sin during it. We belong entirely to You, O God, and, therefore, we offer to You all our thoughts, all our desires, all our words, and all our actions. Be mercifully pleased to inspire and sanctify them by Your grace, and to assist us to accomplish in all things Your holy will.

An act of Faith. O God,

We believe You who are Truth Itself. We believe all that You have revealed, and all that You now teach us through Your Church. We believe because in creation You reveal Your goodness, in Christ You reveal Your love, and in the Holy Spirit You reveal Your abiding presence.   Amen.

An act of Hope. Our Father,

We trust that You will always give us everything that we need, and that You will rule the world with our welfare in mind, because we have been made sons of God through union with Christ, our brother.   Amen.

An act of Love. Our Father,

We love You more than anything in the world because You love us, and because You are perfectly good and holy. We love all our neighbors because we are one with them as we are one with You.   Amen.

Let us implore the protection of our Guardian Angels. O God,

By Your Providence, You have sent Your Angels to guard us. Grant us their continual protection and assistance, so that our voices may be joined with theirs in praising You for all eternity.

Let us consider that this day has been given to us to gain heaven by serving God devoutly, and by loving Him with our whole hearts; let us detest our past sins and particularly those to which we are most inclined; let us carefully avoid all the occasions of sin and take particular resolutions with regard thereto.

My Daily Intercessory Prayer

How can God answer the prayers we address to Him unless we answer the prayers others address to us? Do we answer the prayers of the poor? the maimed? the lame? the sinner? the missionary? If not, then by what right can we expect God to answer our requests?

> *This day in my prayers*
> *I would remember—*
> *Mother and Father*
> *Brother and Sister*
> *Friends and Benefactors*
> *Those who love me*
> *Those who hate me*
> > *without cause.*
> *The Holy Father and His intentions*
> *Mother Church and all her children*
> *My Country and its Chief Executive*
> *The greatest and least of*
> *Its citizens, and especially*
> *Those who in this hour*
> *Are suffering and dying*
> > *in its defense.*
> *People of goodwill that they*
> *May come to the fullness of Faith—*
> *People of evil ways that they*
> > *may be converted.*

The conversion of Russia
and of all the world.
The triumph of God's
Infinite mercy in my life
and in all lives
Through the merits of the
Most Precious Blood
and the intercession of
God's Most Holy Mother.

At the End of the Day

Lord Jesus, we come to You for this evening blessing, to seal within our hearts the inspirations and the memories of this day. We ask You for Your blessing and for the blessing of quietness for every troubled heart, rest for every weary soul, and new faith and courage for all who have faced exhausting tasks this day. We would rest now in You. We are tired, Lord. We would want to find in this evening hour Your stillness and Your peace that bring us into quiet harmony with Your Holy Will. We give You thanks for every challenge that this day has brought, every new vision of God that winged its way across our skies, every whisper of God that we sensed, every thought of God that came in quiet moments, and every need of You that brought us back to You in prayer. So now, dear Father, grant us Your benediction. Watch over us through the hours of darkness. Refresh us in Spirit as well as in body as we sleep. Help us to face the tasks of tomorrow, and may Your holy presence and Your guidance be always before us. Our Lord, bless us.   Amen.

Evening Prayers

*In the name of the Father and of the Son and of the Holy Spirit.
Amen.*

Praised be the Most Holy and Undivided Trinity.

Now and forever.   Amen.

*Let us place ourselves in the presence of God and return Him thanks
for all the benefits we have received, especially during this day.*

We firmly believe, O God, that You are here present, that
You penetrate our most secret thoughts, and that You are
graciously willing to hear our prayers. Grant us the grace to
offer these prayers with so much respect and fervor as to
merit to obtain all their effects. We shall begin them, O God,
by offering You our most sincere sentiments of gratitude for
all the favors both spiritual and temporal that You have
deigned to bestow upon us, especially during this day. Grant
us the grace, O Lord, to feel all their value and to make a
good use of them.

*Let us beg of God the grace to know the sins we have committed this
day and to detest them. Father,*

I have sinned before You; I am not worthy to be called Your
son. You have created me in Your image and called me to a

lofty goal. Yet I have sinned; I have been unworthy of You in my thoughts, words, and deeds—through my fault, through my fault, through my most grievous fault! (Pause for examination of conscience.)

I look up to You,

In the name of Jesus Christ, Your Son, my Lord, who poured out His blood on the Cross for me. Forgive me my guilt, my sins, my selfishness. You are eternal love; take me back into Your heart and hold me fast in Your grace. I want to be and remain Yours. My Lord and my God, my sins are so numerous that I come to You with empty hands . . . I am selfish . . . I think only of myself. And still I would like to be noble and stand before You with an upright heart and an untarnished soul. Mother of God, you looked after the Savior in Nazareth with tender love, help me to be united with Him and to be your faithful son.

Let us ask Mary to help us. We beg your protection,

O holy mother of God. Despise not our petition in our necessity. Free us at all times from every danger, O glorious and blessed Virgin, our Lady, our intercessor, our advocate. Reconcile us with your Son; commend us to your Son; bring us to your Son.

Let us pray for all people. Lord Jesus Christ,

You told us to love our neighbor as ourselves. First of all, then, give us a healthy love of self. Let us realize our worth in Your eyes. Let us recognize our dignity as a child of God. Let us appreciate the many gifts we have received from Your love. Let us see your presence in one another. Help us to be kind to one another. Help us to be patient with one another. Help us to be considerate of one another. Help us to love one another as we love ourselves.

Lord Jesus Christ, bless our families. Be especially generous to our parents for their generosity toward us. Help us to be worthy of them. Hear all their prayers. Bless our brothers and sisters, and all our relatives. May our families be reunited in your loving presence for all eternity.   Amen.

Mercy Prayer

O Lord, have mercy on us! Christ, have mercy on us! Lord, hear my tearful prayer and have mercy on my soul. While I still have time, let the light of heaven take the darkness out of the darkness of my being. I am alone in my darkness, but, O Lord, I fear not.

I know that You are near me always. I trust in Your infinite goodness and mercy. You are the light of the world. Illuminate my sinful being, cleanse me with Your radiance and with everlasting gratitude, I shall sing praises to Your Divine Mercy, forever and ever.   Amen.

Prayer for Cleansing

Dear Jesus, You lifted Your eyes up to heaven once as You were upon the altar of the Cross, and You said the healing prayer, "Father, forgive them for they know not what they do." And You gave that power of forgiving to your apostles and to the disciples who followed in the footsteps of Holy Ordination.

Grant, dear Lord Jesus, that those of us today who approach the tomb of the confessional may leave the old person there and find resurrection. We praise Your name and we glorify You.

Father of all mercy, like the prodigal son, I want to return to You and I say that I have sinned against You. I am no longer worthy to be called Your son, Your daughter.

Christ Jesus, Savior of the world, I pray with the repentant thief to whom You gave absolution, when in that last hour of his existence the grace of the Holy Spirit touched him and his eyes expressed his heart as he recognized the kingdom and kingship of You, Jesus. And all he said, with no excuse for his past behavior, taking full responsibility for his mistakes, as he beseeched Your human Sacred Heart for mercy, was: "Remember me when You go to Your kingdom." Lord Jesus, time was so short and You simply said to him those wondrous words of forgiveness: "This day you and I will have heaven."

O my God, with all my heart, I detest all my sins because they offend You and hurt You. I confess them now, Jesus, and accept the penance Your priest will give to me, knowing full well I deserve just punishment.

But I love You, Jesus, and with a heart filled with holy confidence, I place all my trust in You. You are goodness and mercy! Please send down Your grace upon me so that I may never hurt You again! Thank You, Jesus.   Amen.

Before Confession

Lord Jesus, when You walked this earth, Your whole visage, Your whole personality, Your character, Your traits, Your tendencies, were invitations to people who met You to meet who You really were—the Son of God.

You invited them to read beneath Your actions and Your words, and to know that You came to tell them that the kingdom of God was at hand. You called sinners to Yourself. You gave us the miracle of rebirth through repentance.

Lord, allow us Your grace today, at this moment, the grace of Your merciful Holy Spirit, to avail ourselves of the new birth, the new beginning, the new chapter. Give us a true and pure contrition for all our sins and help us never to offend You again. We ask this through the power of Your passion, crucifixion, death, and resurrection.   Amen.

After Confession

O Lord Jesus, I acknowledge that I have sinned. I also acknowledge that in Your infinite goodness, compassion, and mercy You have forgiven me. I am overwhelmed at the fact. With deepest humility, true sorrow for ever having offended You, and an ever increasing love for You, I kneel now and say, "Thank You, Jesus, for this sacrament of reconciliation."

With the help of Your grace, I shall mend my ways and live in ever closer union with You. I love You, Jesus. Thank You! Amen.

Prayer is a sure and straight arrow
to the waiting heart of Jesus

Song of Praise

O Lord Jesus Christ, I sing Your praises! Raise up on high to the throne of Your glory all endless praise! Hear my feeble voice. My soul is tired, Lord, as it searches for Your presence. My body is weak. My soul is weary. O Lord, I find strength in praising You. Bless me, Lord.

O my people, O you servants of the Lord, sing praise to Him! Bless the Lord all you works of the Lord. Praise and exalt Him above all forever. Angels of the Lord, bless the Lord. You heavens above, bless the Lord. Waters beneath the heavens, bless the Lord. All you hosts of the Lord, bless the Lord. Sun and moon, stars of heaven, every shower, every dew, the winds, the fire, the heat, the ice, the snow, the cold, the rain, the frost, the chill, the nights, the days, light and darkness, bless the Lord. Oh bless the Lord! May Your name be praised forever.   Amen.

In Loving Adoration

Jesus, My God, I bow down in lowliest adoration before You, down to the depths of my utter nothingness. And from that depth, I raise my eyes in humble supplication to Your Sacred Heart, imploring Your mercy and forgiveness for my many sins. Please give me the grace to spend this time of loving reparation in a manner pleasing to You and with all the holy dispositions You desire.

Come into my poor heart Yourself, dear Lord, and work out Your pleasure in it, directing my faculties, my senses, and my powers to Your greater honor and glory. Would that I might console You for all the wrongs Your loving Heart receives from the ingratitude of men!

Holy Mary, Mother of God, chosen by God to be the Mother of His Son, and chosen by His Son to be the Mother of us all, help me to love my God with the purity of your own blessed soul. Dear St. Joseph, all you Angels and Saints, lend me all the love of your hearts, true angelic and saintly love, by which I can love my Jesus as He deserves to be loved. Teach me to pray, to adore, to love, to care, and thus I will find my real honor.   Amen.

To the Holy Spirit

O Holy Spirit, grant us health of mind and body and the fullness of Your grace. Sweet Holy Spirit, we ask You to descend upon each one of us, to fill us with Your gifts. We ask You to possess us, to baptize us in Your Spirit.

O Holy Spirit, we ask You to let us cherish the gift of love, the gift of life, the gift of joy, the gift of peace that comes from accepting You, the Divine Giver of all gifts. Oh give us the contentment that flows from being united with You! Use us to spread our religious experience, to spread the kingdom of praise to the world that needs to be burned with Your Divine Love. Help us, Holy Spirit, to be Your instruments of light to a dark world.   Amen.

Send Your Holy Spirit

Heavenly Father, You have sent Your Son into this world and now He says to us, rather regretfully, "I have come to set fire to the earth, and oh! how I wish it would enkindle!" In the face of that, sweet Jesus, we realize that we are but flickering candles, burned-out torches, illuminating ourselves but not passing on the light and the heat to others.

O God, dear Father, please send forth Your Spirit that we may be enkindled, enflamed, that we may burn with a new fire as a new torch, that we may not be flickering candles but candles of light that will illuminate the whole world.

Oh pray! Let us pray! Oh pray all you angels and saints, that we may be enkindled and go out from the service of this life having done good for the world. Hear our humble prayer, and after this prayer time, may all of us become different children, a different people than we were before. Amen.

For the Gifts of the Holy Spirit

O Holy Spirit, soul of my soul, I adore You! Enlighten me, guide me, strengthen me, console me. Tell me what I ought to do. Help me to be submissive to everything that You permit to happen to me. Show me only what is Your will.

Come, Holy Spirit, fill the hearts of Your faithful. Enkindle in them the glowing fire of Your love. Send forth Your Spirit and You shall be renewed. You shall renew the face of the earth.

O God, who teaches the hearts of the faithful by the light of the Holy Spirit, grant us by that same spirit to have a right judgment in all things and forever to rejoice in this holy comfort.

Come, Holy Spirit, grant me the spirit of WISDOM that I may despise the perishable things of this world and aspire only after the things that are eternal.

Come, Holy Spirit, grant me the spirit of UNDER-STANDING to enlighten my mind with the light of Your Divine Truth.

Come, Holy Spirit, grant me the spirit of COUNSEL that I might ever choose the surest ways of pleasing God and gaining heaven.

Come, Holy Spirit, grant me the spirit of FORTITUDE that I may overcome with courage all the obstacles that oppose my salvation.

Come, Holy Spirit, give me the spirit of KNOWLEDGE

that I may know God and know myself and grow perfect in the science of the saints.

Come, Holy Spirit, grant me the spirit of PIETY that I may find the service of God sweet and amiable.

Come, Holy Spirit, give me the spirit of FEAR, that beautiful spirit of fear of the Lord, so that I may be filled with a loving reverence toward God and may dread in any way to displease Him.

O Holy Spirit, Third Person of the Blessed Trinity, I thank You. I praise You. I love You.   Amen.

Pentecost Prayer

Come, Holy Spirit, come. Fill us with Your power. God, our Father, pour out the gifts of Your Holy Spirit on the world. You have sent the Spirit on Your Church to begin the teaching of the Gospel. Let the Spirit continue the work that You have brought.   Amen.

Prayer to St. Michael the Archangel

Glorious Prince of the Celestial Host, St. Michael the Archangel, defend us in the conflict that we have to sustain "against principalities and powers, against the rulers of the world of this darkness, against the spirits of wickedness in the high places." *[Eph. 6:12]* Come to the rescue of men whom God has created to His image and likeness, and whom He has redeemed at a great price from the tyranny of the devil. It is thou whom Holy Church venerates as her guardian and her protector, thou whom the Lord has charged to conduct redeemed souls into Heaven. Pray, therefore, the God of Peace to subdue Satan beneath our feet, that he may no longer retain men captive nor do injury to the Church. Present our prayers to the Most High, that without delay they may draw His mercy down upon us. Seize "the dragon, the old serpent, which is the devil and Satan," bind him and cast him into the bottomless pit "that he [may] no more seduce the nations."*[Rev. 20:2–3]*   Amen.

Christ the King

Lord Jesus Christ, Son of the Living God, we hail You as our King! We recognize that through You, all things came to be; and in You will all things reach full growth. You are the image of Your Father, the richness of His grace, His free gift to us of life and love. From You, we have received the gift of Your own life to pulse within our spirits and make us truly sons and daughters of God our Father. With God's own love, You loved us, loved us to the end, and You shed Your Blood that we might live. With God's own love, You love us still, risen and in glory.

You share with us Your royal mission to bring the good news to the poor, to proclaim liberty to captives, and to set the downtrodden free.

Lord Jesus Christ, we hail You as our King and pledge to You our hearts and hands to help bring all mankind to Your holy throne and to bring Your boundless love, Your life, Your sacrifice, and the glorious freedom of the children of God to all men.

Sweet Son of the Living God, we welcome You to our hearts. Be the King of our souls! Remain with us, O Lord, and never depart.   Amen.

For Pope John Paul II

God our Father, we ask You to look with mercy and love on Your servant, John Paul II, whom You have chosen to govern Your Church and shepherd Your people. May he through word and through example direct, sustain, and encourage the people in his care, so that with them he may share everlasting life in Your kingdom.

Our Father . . .
Hail, Mary . . .
Glory Be . . . Amen.

Prayer for the Pope, Bishops, and All Clergy

Lord and Savior Jesus, we want to spend this time stepping out in faith to pray for others, to forget ourselves and our own wounds, to set aside our own brokenness for a moment, to pray for that holy man in Rome, that living martyr of humanity, John Paul II. We pray that the word that he proclaims, which is Your word renewed in our time, takes deep root in the hearts of all peoples so that all things may be restored unto Christ.

Lord Jesus, we thank You for not leaving us orphans, for giving us Your sacred Presence in the Eucharist. We thank You for the beautiful gift of priesthood, which You have given to so many men throughout the centuries—the gift of priesthood that we all share.

We thank You for our bishops. May we be an extension of their priesthood to their people, and as this extension, may we display kindness, understanding, forgiveness, charity, honesty, and selfless service to our brothers and sisters.

Inflame the hearts of your clergy, Lord Jesus, with the great knowledge of the powers they possess, both in the natural order raised by grace and the gift of the sacrament they have received. Renew all priests, O Lord, with Your own Divine Priesthood, so that by the living of their lives, they may praise and glorify You and earn home and heaven with You. To You be the power and the glory forever and ever. Amen.

Prayer for Vocations

Heavenly Father, You see the needs of Your people and hear the prayers of Your Church. See our needs for more priestly and religious vocations. Listen to our petitions. We, Your people, need ministers of the word and of the sacrament. We need guides to teach us Your way. We need priests and religious to share Your life with us. Lord, the work in Your vineyard is abundant and the workers are not sufficient.

We ask You to bless our young people with the call to the priesthood of Jesus Christ and the graces needed today in religious life. Enrich this, Your Church, with many holy and zealous priests, sisters, brothers, and deacons. Through them, may all people come to know, love, and serve You more and in a better way.

We ask this through Jesus Christ, Your Son, who lives and reigns with You in the unity of the Holy Spirit now and forever.   Amen.

One must wait upon the Lord. It might take years. Then all the pain and the anguish and the waiting and the suffering for God's sake become a blessing!

When Leaving a Church

Praise You, Jesus! Glorify You, Jesus! Thank You, Jesus! O Jesus my God, Precious Jesus, Jesus my King, Jesus my Love, now I must leave You, but I carry away with me the memory of this moment—the memory of Your wondrous, wounded love. It will not be long until I come to visit You again. Until then, I leave my poor heart before this tabernacle. Let its every beat tell You that I love You and that I am longing to be free to spend another moment with You.

Bless me, Lord Jesus, before I go. Bless my home, my undertakings, my family, my friends, and my enemies too. I will see You soon. I love You.   Amen.

For a Happy Death

My Lord Jesus, I pray for a happy death. I know that death is certain. With You beside me, I shall not be afraid. O Lord and Savior, support me in my last hour by the strong arms of Your sacraments and the fragrance of Your consolation. Let the absolving words be said over me and the holy oil sign and seal me. Let Your own Precious Body be my food, and Your Blood my drink.

May Mother Mary come to me and my angel whisper peace to me and Your glorious saints, my dear patrons, smile upon me so that in and through them all, I may die as I desire to live, in Your Church, in Your faith, in Your grace, and in Your love.   Amen.

For Those to Be Married

Dear Father in heaven, we come before You just as we are. We come in the humanity of our brokenness. It is good for us to know that we are broken people. But You will make us whole. Our love is young and tender. It comes from You. We invite You into our marriage. Stay with us, Lord. Without You we will fumble in this journey together. Grant us a true spirit of Your love. As we reflect conscientiously, we know so well that it is the joy of love we want! Oh how true it is that JOY IS THE HAPPINESS OF LOVE—A LOVE THAT IS AWARE OF ITS OWN HAPPINESS. Pleasure, we know, comes from without. And it is good, too, because You made it to be so. But joy, Lord, THAT is what we want, because joy comes from within our souls and nobody can take it away. It is within the reach of everyone in the world. If there is sadness in our hearts, Lord, it is because there is not enough love. Help us through our married lives to radiate love so that those who meet us will be influenced by Your Holy Spirit of Love dwelling in us. Walk with us through our married days. May our union be a public witness that TO BE LOVED, WE MUST BE LOVABLE; TO BE LOVABLE, WE MUST BE GOOD; TO BE GOOD, WE MUST KNOW GOODNESS; AND TO KNOW GOODNESS IS TO LOVE GOD, AND NEIGHBOR, AND EVERYBODY IN THE WORLD! O Lord, we can learn this only at the feet of Your altar where we make our vows, and where our vows will make us holy.   Amen.

Just as I Am

Lord, I come before You—just as I am. I come to You in the loneliness of my heart. I come to You, Jesus, to tell You that I have renewed my life, here before Your Sacred Presence.

Have mercy on me, Jesus! Have mercy! How I praise You and glorify You. I seek Your strength. I love You, Jesus. Forgive me my sins. Forgive me my weaknesses. Forgive me my brokenness. How I adore You! How I love You! Merciful Jesus, have mercy!   Amen.

Prayer of Surrender

O Jesus, Hidden God, I cry to You!
O Jesus, Hidden Light, I turn to You!
O Jesus, Hidden Love, I run to You!

With all the strength I have, I worship You. With all the love I have, I cling to You. With all my soul, I long to be with You. I fear no more to fail. I shall not fail as long as You stay with me. Oh please never leave me! How I love You, Jesus! How I praise You! How I glorify You! I praise Your name, Lord Jesus, now and forever.   Amen.

A Youth's Prayer

Dear God, give me what it takes to be a holy youth! Give me courage to do what is hard; courage to say NO to sin; courage to hold off the quitter in me. Lord, give me a clean mind and clean speech; let me have clean eyes and clean hands. Help me to cherish cleanliness and to recognize that it brings happiness. Let me appreciate that in purity all things have value.

Dear God, give me the gift of kindness, so I may never hurt another youth. Teach me to control my temper and my tongue, so that they do not become the instruments of cruelty. I know my own importance, Lord, but let me never fail to see that others have importance too.

Grant me strength of spirit to defeat self-pity. If at times I am lonesome, lead me to the knowledge that to be loved I must be lovable; that I will have no real friends until I earn them.

Dear Father in heaven, sometimes it is hard for me to talk to You. I've been a stranger to prayer. But please listen to me. Grant me the bigness I sincerely need to be cheerfully obedient. Remove from my personality a sullen spirit. Teach me to take orders, so that someday I will know how to give them reasonably to others.

Grant me zest and drive to conquer laziness. Never let me feel that I can be served without serving, or get without giving. Instruct my young, tender heart in the love of work, so that I may know the joy of rest.

Dearest Father in heaven, grant that I may long only for You; that I may surrender all other loves for Your sake; that I may surrender any dependencies and addictions to You; and in the paradox of surrendering them to You, because of my love for You, I will be able to learn to love everything with You, for You, and through You.

Grant me the most precious of gifts: that of being able to discern good from evil. May I walk in peace of mind which comes from knowing that I will never lead another to sin. By Your grace, may no one be cheapened because he or she kept my company. Let all who love me learn to love You more! And finally, dear Lord, give me such brightness, laughter, and grace that You will find in me a temple for Your Holy Spirit. So, dear Lord, come into my heart; come to me just as I am. Be my Savior, be my Lord!   Amen.

From a Mother's Heart

God, grant that my little child may instruct me in the way of You. Let his innocent eyes speak to me of the spotless holiness of Jesus. Let his open smile remind me of the great love You have for Your creatures. Let his helplessness teach me Your unbounded power. May his first feeble effort to speak call to my mind the wisdom of the Almighty. May my love for You be stimulated by the deep-rooted affection my child has for me. May I, in all these things, grow in appreciation of my precious holy motherhood.   Amen.

Prayer for My Mother

I thank You, Lord Jesus Christ, for the love of my mother which You have given to me. Of her was I born; through the years when I was helpless she cared for me. Her unselfish love has guided me. Remember her sacrifices, her devotions, her hopes. Lighten her burdens. Give her body and soul the joy of her love for You. You know, O Lord, the secrets of a mother's heart. I pray that my mother who with You and for You has treasured them as her own, may be united, here and hereafter, forever with you.   Amen.

*What counts is not so much the gift you receive,
but what you do with it.*

At the Feet of the Man from Galilee

Lord Jesus, we thank You for bringing us to Your feet, to meet with You, to be with You. You are the Man from Galilee. Lord, give us the grace to respond unconditionally to You. You are calling us to come, to come to Your feet, to sit, to look into Your eyes, into Your soul, into Your heart, into Your being, and to speak with You as You want to speak with us. We will listen, Lord, with all our hearts!

And when we leave Your Presence, we will carry the inner glow of You into the lives of all those whom we meet. Please grant us the grace of a new birth. We ask this through the power of Your Most Precious Blood.   Amen.

An Invitation from Jesus

Come to Me. Come to Me, your Lord. Come to Me with no fear. Come to Me with no limits to what you ask. Come to Me with your weak faith. Come to me with your angry temper. Come to Me with your shivering despondency. Come to Me with your doubts. Come to Me with your hurts and anxieties. Come to Me with all your sickness and disease. Come to Me with your weaknesses and your sins. Above all, come to Me with your love. Come, just as you are, but DO COME! I love you and I am waiting. Oh yes, do come!   Amen.

For Reconciliation

Blessed be the Lord, the God of Israel, for He has visited His people. He has come to rescue, and He has raised up for us a power of salvation. O Lord Jesus Christ, You bless the virtuous and the humble, and You hold contempt for the pride of hypocrites. Help each one of us to be truthful and humble all the days of our lives, and to follow Your example of love. We thank You, Jesus, for giving us the gift of reconciliation. O Lord, I pray in celebration of the fact that God continues to give His gifts of forgiveness and pardon. I pray that I may always be open to receiving these gifts and to be able to say, "Lord, bring us together." O Father in Heaven, You've called us to reconciliation. May we be heeded by all people, as You heed us, and we heed them to You. Let everyone seek the reconciliation, which only God, YOU, can give. Lord, bring us together that the whole Church may be open to renewal and reconciliation, and to healing, and may proclaim throughout the whole world the unity of all humans and Christ. Lord, bring us together!   Amen.

Advent Prayer

O Father in Heaven, help us during this special season to remember the many ways that You have pointed out to us of the coming of our Lord, Jesus Christ. May we be ever mindful that You will not let us sit in darkness. But if we are receptive to Your grace, we will see the light of the many signs that You send us in the Prophets, but especially in the lives of our neighbors and the eyes of our family.   Amen.

Prayer Before Christmas

Lord Jesus, we come before You with love and expectation. Christmas, with all its excitement, its thrills, is already bustling throughout the air and its spirit, Lord Jesus, echoes the spirit of the Word or the spirit of the reality of which You ARE.

Grant each one of us, Lord, whom You have called to partake in this most joyous season by Your Divine Invitation, your Divine Call, the grace to find You—and to continue to find You—in all Your acts of love and in the love of Your children everywhere. Let us return that love, O Lord, during these precious days and all the days of our lives. We ask this through the power of your Sweet Infancy, Holy Childhood, Blessed Adolescence, and through the suffering and death You endured to earn our salvation. We praise You, Our Savior!   Amen

A Christmas Prayer (1)

Lord Jesus, we thank You for the spirit shared abroad in human hearts on Christmas. Will You help each one of us to keep Christmas alive in our hearts and in our homes, that it may continue to glow, to shed its warmth, to speak its message during all the bleak days of winter? May we hold to that spirit, that we may be as gentle and as kindly today as we are on Christmas Eve, as generous tomorrow as we are on Christmas morning.

Then, if by Your help, we should live through a whole week in that spirit, perhaps we may go into yet another week and thus be encouraged and gladdened by the discovery that Christmas CAN last the year round.

So give us, dear Jesus, a joyful, cheerful heart, that we may worship the Lord, our God, with a spirit that is truly Christ-like, the spirit of Christmas.   Amen.

A Christmas Prayer (2)

O Lord Jesus, as we contemplate Your birth in a stable, please receive our Christmas prayer. We pray that strength and courage may be abundantly given to all for the world of reason and understanding, for faith and hope and love, and that the good that lies in every man's heart may day by day be magnified, and that men will come to see more clearly, not that which divides them, but that which unites them. That each hour may bring us closer to a final victory, not of nation over nation, but of man over his own evils and weaknesses. That the true Spirit of this Christmas Season, its joy, its beauty, its hope, and above all its abiding faith may live among us. That the blessing of peace be ours. The peace to build and grow, to live in a harmony and sympathy with others, to plan for the future with confidence.

May Almighty God bless us in the name of the Father, and of the Son, and of the Holy Spirit, and may His peace abound in our hearts.   Amen.

Prayer for Generosity

Dearest Lord, hear my prayer, this prayer for generosity. Dearest, dearest Lord, teach me to be a generous disciple. Teach me to serve You as You deserve, to give and never count the cost; let nothing worry or fear me, and may I fight Your battle without heeding the wounds. Let me toil and not seek rest, let me labor without asking for reward. There is one thing that I do ask, Jesus, and that is to know that I am doing Your will. If you would but grant me Your grace, then I know that I shall be able to know You and to see You more clearly, to love You more loyally, and to follow You more closely.

I should like to learn all this on my knees, for I am certain, that if there *is* one SURE way to You, it is on my knees. I thank You for this privilege and I love You.   Amen.

Doce Me, Domine (Adaptation)

Lord, Jesus Christ, take all my freedom. Take my memory. Take my understanding. And take my will. All that I have and all that I cherish, You have given me. I surrender it all to be guided by Your Will. Your grace and Your Love are wealth enough for me. Give me these, O Lord Jesus, and I ask for nothing more.

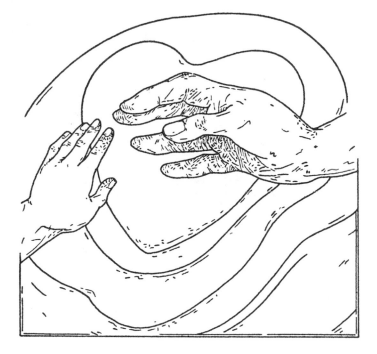

It doesn't take much time to be a saint.
Just a lot of love.

A Lenten Prayer

O gracious God, You are the Father of my Lord Jesus Christ, and also my dear Father. I thank You that You have permitted me to see another Lent with its season of reparation and penance for myself and for others. A period during which I am privileged again to meditate on the Cross of Christ, with its many comforting spiritual lessons. Oh may this Holy Season bring me rich personal blessings, and may the message of the Slain Lamb of God impress upon my heart and mind the awfulness of my transgressions, and the sins of the world, and lead me and others to Calvary for pardon and for peace. O Lord Jesus, lead me to see that my sins and the sins of the world have caused great agony in the garden.   Amen.

Prayer Before a Crucifix

O Lord Jesus Christ, I thank You for dying for me upon the Cross and for shedding Your blood. As I recall Your Passion and Death, Lord Jesus, let me receive Your healing love, Your touch, and forgive me, Jesus, for my indifference. O Lord Jesus, for how many ages since have You hung upon Your Cross with Your arms outstretched.

Still people pass You by and regard You not, except to pierce anew Your Sacred Heart. How often have I passed You by heedless of Your great love. How often have I stood before You, not to comfort and console You, but to add to Your sorrows, to deepen Your wounds, to scorn Your love yet You have stretched forth Your hands to comfort me, to raise me up, and to heal me. I have taken those hands so often, that might have struck me into hell, and I bent them back on the Cross. I nailed them there, rigid and helpless, yet I have but succeeded in engraving my name on Your palms forever. You have loved me with an infinite love, and I have taken advantage of the love to sin and to surrender to my weaknesses, yet my ingratitude has but pierced Your Sacred Heart. Upon me has flowed Your precious blood.

So, Lord Jesus, until the day I die and come to eternity, just let Your blood, Your precious blood, be upon me, not for a curse but for a blessing. O Lamb of God, you take away the sins of the world, have mercy on me. Have mercy on us. Amen.

Easter Prayer

Lord and Savior Jesus, we walk with You now, enjoying the glory and the victory of Your Resurrection. As we walk with You, Lord, we are amazed and astonished at the great manifestation of truth—YOU HAVE RISEN! Now there dwells among us Your resurrected power!

Lord, we live in Your victory, in Your conquest. The shadow of the Cross, however, will always be upon us, until the end of time. Grant, dear Lord, that in each moment of our lives, we may come to rest and bathe in the rays of that Cross.

We pray that in walking in a new birth, in a reconciliation, in righteousness, in a regeneration, we may always turn our hearts and minds away from evil and turn only to virtue and to You, our Savior. We desire nothing more than to walk with You through time and into eternity. It is this that we ask of You, Jesus, through the power of Your passion and death. Amen.

Parents' Prayer for Their Children

O Lord God, You who have called us into the holy state of matrimony and have brought forth the fruit of pure love, thereby making us co-creators with You in the sublime mystery of childbirth, we reverently present to You our dear children.

We entrust them, dear Lord, to Your Fatherly care and all-powerful protection that they may grow daily in wisdom, grace, and love, and be a source of consolation, not only to us who are now privileged to have them, but to You, their Creator, that You may have them forever.

May we look on them as a blessing, as a sacred trust, and as a means of glorifying our married love. May we lead them by kindness and good example, and often recall that they belong to You much more than they belong to us.

And if it be Your Holy Will, we humbly and hopefully ask that at least one of these children be called to Your service.

Lord, be in our hearts and in our home, be in our love and in our children forever.   Amen.

For One's Mother and Father

I thank You, Lord Jesus Christ, for the love of my mother and father whom You have given me. Of them, I was born; through the years when I was helpless they cared for me. Their unselfish love has guided me. Remember, dear Lord, their sacrifices, their devotions, their hopes. Lighten their burdens. Dear Lord, please give their bodies and souls the joy of their love for You. They have been really faithful to You throughout all their years. Their steps are getting heavier now; their hair is grayer; their backs are bent.

You know, dearest Lord, the secrets of a mother's heart, the silent glance of concern of an unpretentious father. Lord, I am praying for my mother and my father that they, who with You, and for You, have treasured Your cause as their own, may be united, here and hereafter, forever with You. Amen.

Families for Prayer

Father, one of Your greatest gifts to us is our family. You have given us to one another to love and to be loved, to care and to share, to learn who we are and what we can become in relationship with You and with one another.

Lord Jesus, You are now calling our family to new depths of personal relationship with You through participation in the Families for Prayer program. Help us to become ever more aware of Your Presence in our home, and help us to respond to You, as a family in prayer. Help our parish family grow in unity and love and help all of us to be that community of prayer to which You call us.

We thank You for the many ways in which You have blessed our family and all the families of our parish. We thank You for having called us together as a community of prayer and worship; for having given us Yourself in the Eucharist to strengthen us and make us one with You and with one another.

We pray in a special way for those families in our parish who most need You: those who are suffering, separated, or alone; those in which there are problems; those who have lost their vision or hope. May the Families for Prayer program lead all of us to a greater awareness of You and of Your love and concern for families. May we be inspired to respond to You in prayer and to reach out to others in love, compassion, and service. Help us to share what we have and what we are with others who have less.

Mary, Mother of Jesus and our Mother, your "yes" at the Annunciation, and throughout your whole life, was a response in faith and trust. Help us, and our parish community, to have that same faith in our response to God and to one another.

Father, may Your Son, Jesus, become ever more a part of our lives, our homes, and our parish. Send Your Spirit to bless and guide us so that through the Families for Prayer program, our family and our parish may respond generously to what You ask of us. We ask this in Jesus' name.   Amen.

For the Nation, State, or City

God our Father, You guide everything in wisdom and love. Accept the prayers we offer for our nation; by the wisdom of our leaders and integrity of our citizens may harmony and justice be secured and may there be lasting prosperity and peace.

We ask this through our Lord Jesus Christ, Your Son, who lives and reigns with You and the Holy Spirit, one God forever and ever.   Amen.

For Those Who Serve in Public Office

Almighty and eternal God, You know the longings of human hearts and You protect human rights. In Your goodness, watch over those in authority, so that people everywhere may enjoy freedom, security, and peace.

We ask this through our Lord Jesus Christ, Your Son, who lives and reigns with You and the Holy Spirit, one God, forever and ever.   Amen.

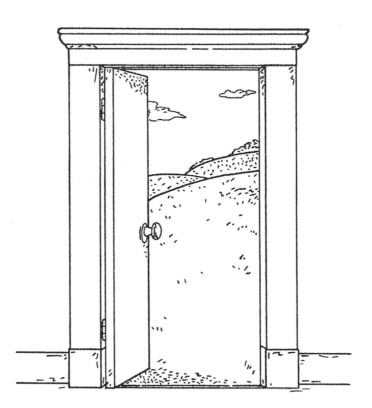

*The foundation of healing
is forgiveness.*

Healing Forgiveness

Lord, You have told us to ask and we will receive, to seek and we will find, to knock and You will open the door to us. I trust in Your love for me personally, and in the healing power of Your compassion. I praise You and I thank You for the mercy You have shown to me. Lord, I'm so sorry for all my sins, my mistakes, my weaknesses. You know me, God, touch me. I ask for Your help. Help me to renounce the sinful patterns of my life. I accept with all my heart Your forgiving love. Lord, hear my prayer. It comes from my heart. I'm sorry, and I ask for your grace, because it's only grace that can change me—nothing else, nobody else. There's no power on earth that can make me great, renewed, reborn, saved, except You. O God, teach me the gift of understanding. Teach me to forgive others; that's the foundation of healing. If I'm going to be healed, I must forgive. I seek Your strength. It's Your strength that brings me peace, Your strength that lets me go on courageously to be an influence of good to others, and to save my own soul. So guide me, Jesus, in this prayer. I thank You, Lord, for hearing me right now.   Amen.

Short Healing Prayer (Rebuking Sickness)

Heavenly Father, we ask that You would hear us in the brokenness of our being, and come to this person right now, and touch this person's life with all Your benefits. Let this person truly know how important he is, what he has cost You: the blood of Your Son, Jesus Christ. And I, God's servant, blessed with the gift of healing, I pray for you, that whatever sickness or disease that's in you be cast out in the name of Jesus, and by the Power of God, the Power of the Holy Spirit. In the name of Jesus, in the Power of the Word, foul sickness and disease, leave this person. Be blessed and be healed in the name of the Father, and of the Son, and of the Holy Spirit.   Amen.

A Prayer When Tired

O Lord Jesus, look upon me with kindness as I come to You at this moment. I want to rest a while. I need to feel Your strength, Your warmth, Your love. Place me close to Your Heart. Place Your arms about me. Breathe Your Spirit into me. Give me the grace and the strength to rise from the frailty and pettiness of my humanity.

Give me the grace also, through the power of Your Holy Spirit, to become truly Your brother, Your sister, and bring me, Lord, to the Father. O Father, time passes rapidly and I hear the chimes of the clock of time. It bids me to recognize that I have a soul to be saved—to be saved NOW.

Save me, O Lord, for You are my Savior! I thank You, my sweet Lord. I shall sing Your praises forever.   Amen.

Your Will Be Done

Our Father, You are our God. Each one of us comes to You with closed eyes but with open hearts, well realizing that what You desire for us is so much better than what we want for ourselves. For, as the heavens are far above the earth, so are Your ways higher and better than our ways. Help us to be motivated and to be healed. Help us to realize that it is far better to be deep and to be narrow, and we are close to You. O Lord Jesus Christ, show us the way that we may joyfully fulfill Your plan for us. Oh what victory, what glory, what celestial, heavenly, infinite, prospect God has reserved in store for us who love Him. Bless us. Yes, bless us each day, dear God, as we go our way.   Amen.

Invocation

Oh comfort all those in need, my God, with Your forgiveness of their sins, of our sins, and grant us patience in suffering all the problems of life until in Your wisdom, in Your gracious providence, all of us may be restored to health again. Let the glory of Your name be ever proclaimed to the world. O God, hear our prayer.

My God and Savior, O Lord Jesus Christ, just lead me in Your way, that I may walk in Your truth. Gladden all our hearts that we may fear Your holy name. O Lord, You are so mighty in Your mercy, so gracious in Your might. Assist each one of us. Comfort us, save us, save me. We put our trust in Your holy name. Jesus, Holy Jesus, have mercy on us. In Your wrath, do not let us perish.

O Lord, You are the lover of humanity. Show me, show us, Your great mercy, Your compassion. O physician, healer of my soul, of our souls, merciful Savior, blot out all our transgressions from the depth of Your heart. You have brought us to it, to Your woundedness. You who are a wounded healer receiving a wounded seeker. Almighty one, stay close to us. Help us to avoid evil ways. Give us new strength. Keep us under Your protection, under the shadow of Your wings, so that I, we, the human race, may serve You faithfully.

Praise You, glorify Your name all the days of my life. O Father, this is my hope. Hope that was brought to us through Your Son, Jesus Christ, who is our refuge, and the Holy

Spirit, our shelter. O Holy Trinity, may all glory be to You. All my hope I place in You, through Mary, the Mother of God. Keep us now, forever, under Your protection. Amen.

I Believe in Miracles

Graciously heal their bodies, Father. Jesus, wash them with Your precious blood. Holy Spirit, descend into their very beings. Refresh their souls with Your comfort, Your presence, that being restored to health, Your people healed may render thanksgiving forever to You in Your Church, and the heavens. This we ask through Jesus Christ, Your Son, Our Lord. For those who believe, there is no need for an explanation. For those who do not believe, an explanation is not possible. Nothing is impossible with God!   Amen.

Emotions

Lord Jesus Christ, I come before You just as I am, with my nothingness. I ask You that out of this nothingness You will make a new creation, You will cleanse me, in Your precious blood, from all my sins. I ask that You will heal me in my spirit, that You will inculcate within me more faith, more hope, and more love. I ask You, Lord Jesus Christ, to heal me in my soul, to cleanse me of all the inordinate surrenders of my emotions of love, hate, anger, sadness, joy, fear, jealousy, and boldness. My Lord Jesus Christ, I surrender myself to You with my broken body. Lord Jesus Christ, I give myself to You forever.   Amen.

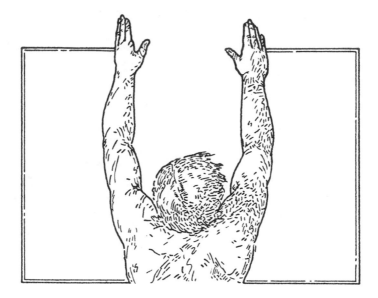

Don't run away from your passions, your weaknesses, your humanity. Give your humanity to Jesus. Place it in His hands.

Be Open

Lord Jesus Christ, I come before You. I want to be Your clear channel of healing grace to my brother and to my sister. I ask You at this very moment to cleanse me of any negativism, to deliver me from anything that may hinder the healing power of Christ in my brother and sister.

Lord Jesus Christ, I thank You for the healing power that You are giving to us, Your children. I wash myself in Your Holy Blood. I ask, dear Jesus, that You will send Your Holy Spirit of healing upon us who are sick of spirit, of soul, or of body.   Amen.

For Insight

Oh, staying with grace is staying with You, my Lord. You are the one who refreshes and makes me new, who makes my day new, who lessens my fascination with futile things and awakens me to only what counts. Keep touching me inwardly, Lord, until the light of insight dawns. Do not allow the flicker of light to die before it becomes a living flame consuming me. Make me treasure, Lord, the dawn that grows in me. Make me dwell on the voice that speaks inaudibly. Make me cherish the moment of illumination. Dispose me to the tender beginnings of Your inspiration. Be an oasis in the desert of my life. Still the noise of daily chatter, that I may hear anew the murmur of Your living waters. God, speak to me. Refine me. Enlighten me. Bless me.   Hallelujah.

Pride and Vanity

Oh bless me, Father, for I have sinned. O Christ, my God, I now stand before You in the presence of all Your holy angels, as if I were standing before Your fearful and just judgment throne, rendering an account of all my evil deeds and awaiting Your sentence. O Jesus, I place myself before You, before time closes itself to me. Heal me, Lord, and make me one with You. Forgive me my sins of vanity, my sins of pride, my sins of slander, my idle speech, my unkind laughter, my intemperance, my hatred, my envy, my jealousy, my selfishness, my ambition. Yes, perhaps even my falsehood. O my God, bless me!

Heal me, Lord Jesus. O my God, my Lord Jesus Christ, lead me to Your wounded heart and heal me. Lead me in Your way that I may walk in Your truth, gladden my heart that I may feel Your holy name. Assist me, comfort me, save me. I put my trust in Your holy name. O Lord, my God, You are the lover of mankind. Show me that You'll heal me. Show me Your great mercy, Your compassion. O Physician, O Healer of my soul, O merciful Savior, blot out my transgressions. In the depth of my heart, I am truly sorry for having offended You. Grant me now Your grace, that I may avoid my earlier and evil ways.

Give me Your strength, Almighty One, to conquer the temptations of life, to overcome my weaknesses—especially pride and vanity. Keep me under Your protection and under the shadow of Your wings, that I may serve You faithfully. I praise You and glorify Your holy name all the days of my life. Amen.

Prayer of Faith in Time of Suffering

Lord Jesus Christ, how I love You. How we love You. In Your earthly life You performed many miracles of healing and yet You suffered Yourself for our salvation. This mystery of health and of suffering seems a paradox. You indicated in Your own words the paradox is solved by faith. O Lord, just grant us the faith to believe in the power of healing today. Help us to recognize Your merciful power in the hands of the physician, in the words of the psychiatrist. Help us especially to see Your healing miracle in the anointing given by a Priest in the Sacrament of the Sick. Help us to believe in the possibility of supernatural cures, be they physical, emotional, psychological, or spiritual in nature. Help us to believe in Your providence and in Your desire for our well-being.

Lord, grant us the faith to see how human suffering can be a participation in Your own suffering. Help us to realize that the crippled, the blind, the lame, the mentally deficient, all serve to bring salvation to the world by uniting their suffering with Your own. Help us, Lord, too, to realize that our own suffering can serve as expiation for sin, and thus contribute to man's salvation. Finally, Lord, reconcile us within ourselves by granting us the gift of health and reconcile us to the Father's will in helping us to accept the gift of suffering. I pray this, Lord Jesus, in faith.

O Lord Jesus, we ask You to bless all the doctors and nurses who give their lives for the sick. Lord, You are the

Heavenly Physician. You are able to give health to the body, wholesomeness to the mind, and peace to the soul. So work, dear Jesus, Your mystery. Your mystery of love through the ministry of mercy—in all the hospitals, in the nursing homes, in rehabilitation centers, and so on throughout the whole world. Bring Your healing to all the distressed.

Give doctors and nurses patience and wisdom as they minister to the needy. Grant everyone a special measure of love and understanding toward those who are frightened and in pain. Walk with doctors and nurses and priests through the corridors of our hospitals and enter every room with Your tender mercy and Your healing care.

Use us, Lord Jesus, to bring hope and courage to the lonely, to the discouraged. Give opportunities, Lord, for us to speak a word for You and of You. Lord Jesus, bring healing love to all mankind. Heal us, Lord Jesus. We ask this in Your holy name.   Amen.

For Understanding

Teach me, Lord, to be kind and patient in all the events of daily life, the disappointments, thoughtlessness of others, insincerity of those I trusted. Teach me, Lord, to profit by the sufferings that come across my path each day. Let me so use them that they may mellow me, not harden or embitter me. Make me patient, not irritable, broad in my forgiveness, not proud and narrow and overbearing. Teach me, Lord, to whisper a word of love to You as I meet with one cross after another. May my life be full of power for good, and may it be strong in its purpose of sanctity.   Amen.

Song of My Soul

O Lord Jesus Christ, it is not what I am, but what You are that counts. How true. Not what I am, Lord, but what You are. That and that alone can be my soul's true rest. Your love, not mine, makes this fear and doubt depart, and stills the tempest within me. It blesses now and it shall forever bless. It saves me now, and shall forever save. It holds me up in days of helplessness. It bears me safely over each swelling wave. 'Tis what I know of You, my Lord and my God, that fills my soul with peace and my lips with song. You are my health, my joy. You are my staff, my rod. Leaning on You, Jesus, in weakness, I am strong. Oh more of Yourself, O Lord. Not what I am. Oh show me hour by hour more of Your glory. O my God and my Lord, more of Yourself. Give me more of Yourself, O God, in all Your grace and power. Give me more of Your love and Your truth, for You are the Incarnate God. O Jesus, I realize that there are people around the world who are far greater in need of me to pray for them than I am to pray for myself. Keep me aware, Lord, of the world's needs, as You are aware of them. Listen to all of us, Lord, and heal us now and always.   Amen.

Anima Christi (Adaptation)

O Soul of Christ, make me holy.
O Body of Christ, be my salvation.
O Blood of Christ, let me drink Your wine.
O Water flowing from the Side of Christ,
*   wash me clean.*
O Passion of Christ, strengthen me.
Kind Jesus, hear my prayer.
Hide me within Your Sacred Wounds.
Defend me from every evil.
And call me at my death to
Your fellowship and to Your
*   saints in Heaven.   Amen.*

For My Sins

Forgive me my sins, O Lord. Forgive me the sins of my youth. Forgive me the sins of my age, the sins of my soul, and the sins of my body. Forgive me, O Lord, for my secret sins, my whispering sins, my presumptions, my sins of omission, and my sins of commission. The sins that I have done to please myself and the sins that I have done to please others. O my God, forgive me as You heal me. Forgive me those sins that I know, and those sins I know not of. Forgive them, Lord, forgive them all out of Thy great goodness.   Amen.

"The more you are forgiven, the more you will love."

Out of the Depths, I Cry to You, O Lord

O my God, I need You. I need You now. I know that I can do nothing without You. I know that I can do without many of the things that once I thought were necessary, but without You, my God, I cannot live. I dare not die. I needed You when sorrow came, when shadows were thrown across the threshold of my life, and You did not fail me. Not then, nor will You fail me now. I needed You when sickness laid a clammy hand upon my family, upon me. I cried to You and You heard me. Hear me now, O God, as I consecrate my life to You in time and eternity.   Amen.

Come, Lord

O God of Mercy, God of Might, with whom nothing is impossible, and whose delight is to come to the aid of the afflicted, the distressed, the sick, the suffering, and those who come to services seeking hope from their God, whom are we to turn to, O God, except to You, to Thyself! Oh come, Father, come to the afflicted, come to the distressed. Show Yourself to that special person who is reading this, that special person, God, who needs Your Grace, Your healing love of Spirit, for soul and body. Oh comfort them, Jesus. Comfort that woman, comfort that man, young or old. Comfort that teenager who is striving to find himself, the purpose of his existence. O God, come with the blessed assurance of the forgiveness of their sins and the blessed assurance that they will receive health. O God, in Your wisdom, Your gracious providence, the world can be renewed. O God, send Your power now upon us, and Your love. We ask this through Jesus Christ our Savior, the wounded healer.   Amen.

The Lord Has Pardoned

Dear Lord, I humbly thank You for sending Jesus Christ to take away all my sins. I realize that since Adam and Eve were driven out of Your presence because of their sins I have been separated from You by my iniquities, but now I confess all my sins to You. I humbly ask Your forgiveness. I believe Jesus died for me and shed His blood for the remission of my sins. You promised total pardon if I would believe in Your Son, Jesus Christ. I do believe now. I do accept, by faith, full pardon for every sin. I believe the blood of Jesus Christ, which was shed on that Cross, is cleansing me now. I believe that in Your great mercy and love You died for me as my substitute. I believe that You suffered all the penalty of my sins and that You paid the full price, so that there is no more sin laid to my charge. You were perfectly innocent. You did no wrong. I was the sinner. I broke God's rule. I should have been crucified, but You loved me too much to let me die for my own sins. O Lord Jesus, I thank You for taking my place, for paying my full debt. Your precious blood was shed for the remission of my sins. I surrender to You, my Lord Jesus Christ, my whole being, all my sins, my body, my soul, my heart, my all.   Amen.

For the Gift of Presence

Dear Father in Heaven, You love Your children, You love Your world, You love every nation. You have made us out of nothing, and at every moment of our existence, that existence which You gave us, You are present to us, Father, present to us in gentle understanding, and gentle compassion in mercy and in love. Your arms are always open to us. O Father, how we love You. Thank you for being a Father. Thank you for the gift of life. Thank you for the Church. Thank you for the gift of supportive friendship. Just help us to be present to one another, so that our presence may be a strength that heals the wounds of time and gives hope that is for all persons. We ask this through Jesus Christ our Lord and Brother.   Amen.

An Offering of Faith

O dear Father in Heaven, we ask for miracles upon all of Your children. Through Scriptures and as we see through the experience of time and centuries past, Your promise is true. We place our faith in You and You alone. O Father, through Your Holy Spirit, through Your Son, Your Christ, the Jesus, the Wounded Healer, we bring our broken bodies. We bring the bodies of men that have become diseased through sickness and time and circumstances. We bring our souls with all their emotions of love, hate, sadness, joy, boldness, anger, fear, and desire. We bring all these to You. We bring our spiritual life to You. We ask You to inculcate within each one of us more faith, more loyalty, more hope in the great expectation of Your promise, more unity with love. O Lord, we bring our weakness, the frailties of our humanity. O God of mercy, stretch out Your hand and grant healing to all of us who are sick in some fashion or some form. Heal us, Lord Jesus. Heal us that we may be one. Be always by our side. Be our helper and never forsake us, Lord, and never despise us.   Hallelujah!

Intercessory Prayers

O Father in Heaven, at every moment of our existence You are present to us. Present to us in gentle compassion. Help us, Father, to be present in supportive friendship to one another both near and far away, so that our presence may become a strength that heals the wounds of time. That our thoughts and words and reflections may be given to all. All, that is, for all persons. For all creeds, for all nations. With the psalmist we cry out, "Heal me, O Lord, that I may be healed. Save me, that I may be saved. For it is in You that I find life and salvation. It is You whom I praise. Heal my soul, God. Heal my spiritual being, and heal my body from sickness, disease, and decay." O Father, You are the God of mercies. Stretch out Your hand and grant healing to all that are sick, and make us have faith in Your promise. Make us be worthy of the blessing of renewed health.   Amen.

Almighty and most merciful God, You are the great physician, and all of us come before You with a prayer in behalf of ourselves and for those who are close to us and for the whole world. O God, you know all those who lie in dire need of Your divine health. You know the pain, the danger, the temptations which have befallen every man, woman, and child. You alone can provide the relief, the help, which will perfectly answer the needs that here present themselves by the human race.

We beseech You, Lord, with full confidence in Your love and power that You may graciously behold and visit and relieve all the distressed: little children, abused children, lonely children, suffering children, sick children: also abused adults, lonely adults, and those experiencing emptiness and pain of all kinds. Grant the whole world, Lord, the joy of Your praise and love. Grant them, Lord, the joy of praising You, that they may see You. May Your hand touch them and heal them. Grant them deliverance from sickness and disease, from contagion, from evil influences.

Teach us all to value health and strength. O God, Your precious gift is life and supportive friendship. O God, You are the eternal salvation of every man, woman, and child. Hear our prayers, Lord, in behalf of all Your servants who are sick, for whom we implore Your aid, the aid of Your mercy. Heal their bodies. Heal them, Lord, refresh their souls with comfort, that being restored to health they may render thanks to You, in Your Church, through Jesus Christ, the Son of God.   Amen.

General Intercession

Lord Jesus, we pray for the Church, for the Holy Father, for priests and bishops, for all the ministers of religion who serve You with faith, with hope, with love, with sincerity, truth, and sacrifice. We raise them up, Lord Jesus, to Your heart that they may preach You—Jesus Christ—and teach You by their lives. Protect our sovereign Pontiff and all the bishops and priests united with him.

Dear St. Joseph, protector of the Church and family life, we ask you to intercede for the Church and for us. We also ask you to grant us a happy death, a peaceful death, a death where we might die in the arms of Christ, in the arms of the Church who gives us the sacraments.

Lord, we want to pray for those who need to find work, the unemployed.

We want to pray for the hungry, Lord Jesus. You urged us to feed the starving of the world, Lord, for in the hunger on their faces can be seen Your hunger. Help us to be compassionate. Help us to find Your kindness within our own souls. We know that there are millions of Your children, our human family, who are dying of hunger. Do not allow us to remain indifferent to their crying need or to numb our consciences.

Lord, we pray for those who are dying today. Remember Your own fear and agony and have mercy on them.

Protect all who are making journeys today by air, sea, or land, and grant them a safe arrival.

We pray for international organizations and governments, for city, state, and national officials. We pray for all Your people, Lord Jesus, that they may become "one."

Bless all our friends and relatives, my Lord. While You were on earth, You had close and devoted friends such as John, Lazarus, Martha, and Mary. In this way You showed us that friendship is one of life's greatest blessings. We want to thank You for our friends, for those who love us, for those whom we love. Let me ever behave toward them as You behaved toward Your friends and bind us together, Lord, in You. Oh bind us, Lord Jesus, bind us together.

Lord Jesus, we pray for those who study—young students, old students, students of colleges and universities, students of all schools. We pray, too, for those who teach Christian doctrine, that they may teach Jesus Christ and His truths.

We pray now also for priests leaving their religious vocations. Let us not judge but instead take a look at our own consciences. Grant us the ability to see Your precepts and commandments more clearly. Give all Your priests, Lord Jesus, the dignity to uphold their priesthood, and give them the grace to uphold their call. Renew within them a spirit of holiness. Go to the lonely missionaries. Watch over them, all your religious, and the lay people who leave everything to give testimony to Your word and Your love. When they experience those difficult moments that are so frequent, give them Your holy energy and strength. Comfort their hearts. Crown their work with spiritual achievements.

Lord, we pray for unity of Your Church, of Your people. You have asked that Your Church be one, Your people be one, as You are one with the Father. Christians have not been united, Jesus. We have isolated ourselves from one another. We have misunderstood and ridiculed and have even gone so far as to attack one another. In so doing, Jesus, we have offended You. We have added to Your pain and anguish. Lord, help us stop this scandalous disunity. Forgive us. Enlighten us that we may see the path that leads to You. Strengthen us,

Lord, and our wills so that we may build up Your Church. Blot out our sins. Renew our minds. Heal our bodies. Enkindle our hearts and guide us by Your Holy Spirit into the grand "oneness" which is Your will. And, Jesus, slow us down. We praise You, Father, and we glorify You.

Amen.

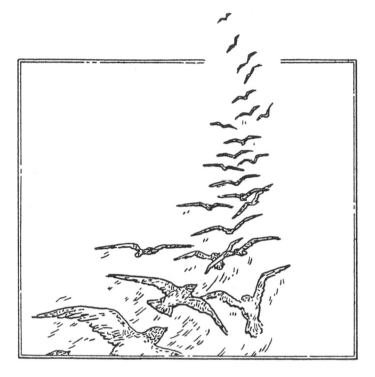

"*The man who thinks only of himself, says prayers of petition. He who thinks of his neighbor, says prayers of intercession. He who thinks only of loving and serving God, says prayers of abandonment to God's will, and that is the prayer of the Saints.*"

(FULTON J. SHEEN)

Hymn to Mary

O Mary, Mother of God, You stand beneath the Cross of Your Son, Jesus Christ, as He hangs there like a living chalice of salvation with His blood flowing out so copiously, so rapidly upon us, upon the world. We are soaked in the Lamb Jesus' blood. O Mary, You were chosen by Your God, by Your Father, to be the Mother of Your Son, and so You became the Immaculate Virgin, and You became the Mother of Divine Providence. Keep my soul, keep our souls pure and holy. Keep it with the fullness of God's Grace. Govern my life. Direct it in the way of virtue, of temperance, control, of dignity for my humanity, for my spiritual life. God created me for Him. Lead me to the fulfillment of God's divine will. Obtain for me the pardon, the remission, of all my sins. Be my refuge, be my protection, be my defense, be my guide in my pilgrimage through this world. Oh comfort me in the midst of tribulation, storms, and adversity. O Mary, O Mother of God, God gave You these gifts to serve His children. Obtain for me, O Mary, the renewal of my heart within me, that I may give myself a new commitment to Your Son, Jesus Christ. O Mary, I love You. I pray to God. I ask You, Mary, to bless me, intercede for me. Hallelujah, hallelujah, hallelujah.

Asking Mary's Intercession

Holy Mother of God, how we love your Son! How very often choices are given to us and how very often these choices would be pleasing to our human nature. But, dear Mary, as we move and as we are moved by the forces of our humanity, there comes the moment of the conscious choice of recognizing who God is and who we are.

And, O Sweetest Mother, we choose Jesus, your Son. We want to give Him our spirit, our mind, our body, our whole being. Dear Mary, intercede for us. Ask Jesus to come to us, enrich us, preserve us, and live in us. May He be the one and true source of our existence.

Blessed Mother of God, we consecrate ourselves to Jesus through you, just as we are. Have pity on us as we strive to create a new life for your Son, our Savior. Remain close to us so that we may steadfastly fulfill what we have set out to do. Then one day in heaven, along with all the angels and saints, we may honor and praise you forever as Our Mother, Queen of Heaven.   Amen.

To Jesus Through Mary

O Mother of Mercy, You are also the help of all Christians, You are most faithful to God's plan. God made You the treasure of all Grace through the title Co-redemptrix. Remember that never in the world has it been heard that You would leave Your children comfortless. O Mary, because of this I trust in Your tender pity. O Mary, intercede for us. Pray for us. We praise You, we glorify You, we honor You, because God made You His Holy Mother. Teach us the true meaning of adoration, commitment, and surrender. Obtain for us God's forgiveness from the Cross. Allow us to surrender ourselves to Him and to be healed by Your Son, the Wounded Healer.   Amen.

To Mary, Help of the Sick

O Mary, You suffered with Your Son, Jesus Christ. You offered the sacrifice of Him to the Father, for us who are sick and diseased. O Mary, if you had been separated from Your Divine Son, like a quiet peaceful garden with the sun playing on it, far away from the storm that enveloped the glory of Calvary, You would never have been our Mother. How terrible the sea of human sorrows would be without Your moonlight shining upon it, but now that you are called to suffer with our Redeemer, you become the Mother of the afflicted.

O Mary, wipe away our tears, for You understand sorrow. Mend our broken hearts, for Yours was broken. Draw out all swords, for the hilt is in Your hand. O Mary, You are the Mother of Sorrows, but, Mother, if You were not, then You could never bear the cause of our joy. O Mary, intercede for the sick. Those who are suffering with tumors. O Mary, those who are suffering with eye disturbances, the blind; those with lung cancer, with terminal heart conditions.

O Jesus, Jesus, heal those who are suffering with alcoholism or drug addiction. May Your name be praised and glorified, O Jesus, and may the sorrows of Mary touch the sorrows of everyone and give us the hope, for Mary is our hope. Amen.

Prayer of Abandonment

O Mother, if the assaults of life have wounded me and I must fall, O Mother, then let me indeed fall, but fall into Your protecting arms. Once safely there, our Father above will not reject me. But looking at me in Your arms, He will think and remember that He once put the Child Jesus into Your arms in Bethlehem for love of me. Then, dear Mother, I will not fear to die, for then in dying I will die to myself, my sins. I will live forever in the Angelic House of Heaven where God reigns supreme. You are Queen, and Jesus is my King. O dearest Mother, death, with its sting, will have no effect but will be the key to eternal bliss in an agelessness of eternity. In the name of the Father, and of the Son, and of the Holy Spirit.   Amen.

Prayer of Intercession to the Mother of God

O Virgin Mary, Mother of God's children, Mother of the Church, Mother of the sick, Refuge of sinners, help all who come to You. By the special privilege of becoming the Mother of God, You were filled with the Holy Spirit—the fullness of degree; You became the Immaculate Conception. God gave You the privilege of the Assumption. O Christ bearer, O Mother of Christ, by Your prayers You continue to deliver our souls from death, because You intercede for us with a maternal love, and neither the tomb nor death could hold You. You, who are constant in prayer, even now as You are in heaven! Yes, God has permitted You to be our firm hope as You intercede for us, Your children. We thank You for being the Mother of Life, for being the "Woman of Courage," for becoming the Christ bearer. Oh yes, Mary, You certainly deserve to be translated to life. To live with God the Father, the Creator; to live with the Holy Spirit, Your Spouse. O Mary, we pray through the one who dwelt in Your virginal womb, Jesus. He has crowned You Queen of heaven and of earth! O Mary, Mother of the Church, intercede for us.   Amen.

Prayer of a Young Man

O Mother Mary, Your Son, Jesus, got his first lesson in courage when He saw You smiling gallantly one wintery night in spite of poverty and cold, and despite the fact that people had refused You a house, giving You a stable instead. No wonder He was brave in the face of blustering men and roaring tempers. May I have a little of His courage which was largely Yours? I've got to be pure in believing. Purity, Mother, is something You understand, as no one else does. We young men learned to love at first through the eyes of our own mothers, then Yours when we lifted up to kiss the "Madonna." Purity and motherhood are so closely linked that we can't be unclean without implicit contempt for motherhood and scorn of our own mothers and You. Women, I've been taught, are Your daughters. You've got to help me always to remember that. When a girl is sweet and fine, I want to leave her just that way. When she isn't, perhaps my respect for her will make her feel a little different. O Mother, I need a brother. You know I need guidance and help and a leader whom I can trust and follow with inspired loyalty. So, Mother, the one I need is Your Son, and my elder brother, Jesus Christ. You gave Him to the world. Give Him to me now for my companion, for my friend, and for my leader. Whatever my life might be, I want to walk through it with Jesus at my side. O Mother, Woman of Women, be close to me always.   Amen.

Memorare

Remember, O Most Gracious Virgin Mary, that never was it known, that anyone who fled to Your protection, implored Your help, or sought Your intercession was left unaided. And so, inspired with this confidence, I fly unto You, O Virgin of Virgins, my Mother. To You do I come. Before You I stand, sinful and sorrowful. O Mother of the Word Incarnate, despise not my petitions, nor the petitions of the Broken Body of Your Son, Jesus, but in Your mercy hear and answer me. Amen.

"To become Christlike should be our only ambition in this world. It is the greatest of all aspirations."

Prayer to the Trinity

Eternal Father, loving God, You made each one of us right from the dust of the earth. Transform us now by the Spirit's grace which You sent on that glorious day of Pentecost. Give value, right now, to our little worth, our nothingness, our emptiness. Just prepare each one of us for that day of days when Christ, from Heaven, will come with might and power. He will come to call each one of us out of the dust again, and our bodies will become glorified in light.

O Godhead, Father, Son, and Holy Spirit, how untouched, unseen You are. But all things that are created bear Your trace, the seed of glory that is sown in man. It will flower when we will see Your face. O Father, just turn our eyes to Your Son, Jesus Christ. May He lead us in our faith and bring us to perfection. Father, please give us Your strength.

We pray for cheerfulness and a generous heart. May each one of us bring joy to our homes, to our work, and to all whom we meet. We pray for all who are working today, Lord, and those who will work tomorrow; and for those who do not have jobs, God, open up a path of livelihood for them. Be with them in their homes, in their towns, in their cities, in their factories, in their shops, in their churches, in their fields. Lord, we pray for those who have no work.

We pray for the disabled, for the sick in hospitals and nursing homes, those closest to eternity, those who will die today. For those who cannot find You, Jesus. We pray that through their perplexities and problems of life, You will shine and give them the path to You. O Father in Heaven, we pray for the retired, for the aged. Stay with us, Lord, on our journey of life. Help us to realize that our troubles are slight and short-lived. They're really nothing compared with the joy we shall have when we reach our home in Heaven with You. So come to the lonely, come to the unloved, those without friends. Show them Your love and help them to care for their brothers and sisters. Take away our pride, our temper, our anger. May we follow You in Your gentleness, and may You make us humble of heart.

Give us the faithfulness and the fullness of Your Holy Spirit. Remember, Lord, remember Your solemn covenant. We renew it now through the blood of Jesus Christ. We, Your people, come before You with our nothingness, for Your grace.   Amen.

For God's Continued Presence

Send your blessings, O Lord, upon each and everyone of us who seek the sustenance of daily bread. Enrich our minds that we may know Your personal Providence for our welfare. Encourage our wills that we may pursue Your paths for our earthly walk. Strengthen our bodies that we may physically accomplish our daily needs. Thus blessed in Your grace, we may pass our earthly existence in accord with the human dignity You have bestowed on us.   Amen.

When Depressed

O Father, there are times in life when our souls are filled in oppressive disquiet. Yes, occasionally we can trace these moods of depression to a specific cause. There are other times when we just cannot find the exact reason for our depression, for our despair. We try to find answers from psychology and philosophy and all the techniques that are human. But, Lord, when we come down to it, there has to be some form of lack of faith, hope, and love. So, Lord, if we sit down and we think, we try to remember what it is that has upset us so. We may realize that our depression is based on something unkind that we may have done to another person whom we love. We love them. Be they far or be they near. Our sin may be large in our own mind. So large that we fear that our Savior will never forgive us. Our faith trembles as we think that we will not be able to come to Him. So, Jesus, it is important to remember that God put His Son here on earth, that He could offer us the forgiveness we all need. O Jesus, You will not turn from us, because You love us. Thank you, Jesus, for lifting our sagging spirits and for showing us the Light.   Amen.

God's Unfailing Love

Almighty God, You really are the refuge of all who are distressed and depressed. Just grant unto us that in all troubles of this, our mortal life, we may flee to the knowledge of Your loving us with kindness, loving us with Your tender mercy, that so sheltering ourselves within this trust, this assurance, the storms of life, the perplexities will be passed over us. They would not shake the peace of God that is within us. Whatsoever this life may bring us, grant that it may never take from us the full faith that You are our Father. Grant that we always have life through Your Son, Jesus, and bless all our loved ones, far and near.   Amen.

For a Troubled World

O Father, in our brokenness we come to You. O our Father, You are the giver of all good. You are the sharer of our sorrows and our joys. Just grant us the wisdom, the knowledge, to pray with hearts that are subdued with Your love. Even though this world reels with wars and wickedness, and with the wreckage of sin, yet we know that Your plans fail not. Help us today to be part of the solution to the problems of life and not part of the problems themselves. O Father, may Your love today extend to every human heart, to the soldiers wounded and dying on the battlefield, to the little child crying in the ghetto, to the starving refugee, to the governor, to the presidents of the great corporations, to the humble housewife, and to the breadwinner. Bring to each Your measure of strength, which is essential to living the life of victory for You.   Amen.

Healing Prayer

Lord Jesus, in Your earthly life You performed many miracles of healing and yet suffered Yourself for our salvation. This mystery of health and suffering seems a paradox. You indicated in Your own words that the paradox is solved by faith.

Lord, grant us the faith to believe in the power of healing today. Help us to recognize Your merciful power in the hands of the physician and in the words of the psychiatrist. Help us especially to see Your healing miracle in the anointing given by a priest and in the sacrament of the sick. Help us to believe in the possibility of supernatural cures, be they physical, emotional, psychological, or spiritual in nature. Help us to believe in Your providence and in Your desire for our well-being.

And, Lord, grant us the faith to see how human suffering can be a participation in Your own salvific suffering. Help us to realize that the crippled, the blind, the lame, the mentally deficient, all serve to bring salvation to the world by uniting their suffering with Your own. Help us, too, to realize that our own suffering can serve as expiation for sin, and thus contribute to human salvation. Finally, Lord, reconcile us within ourselves by granting us the gift of health, and reconcile us to the Father's will in helping us to accept the gift of suffering. I pray in faith, Lord Jesus.   Amen.

Healing Prayer for Wholeness

Lord Jesus Christ, by Your healing might, by Your healing power, just enter into our bodies and flow down through us to heal anything that is wrong with our heads, with our eyes, with our ears, with our mouths. Also anything that is wrong with the neck region, Jesus, or the shoulders. Straighten any backs out right now, Lord Jesus, that need healing, scoliosis (curvature of the spine), disc disturbances, Jesus. We just have to be quiet right now, and we pray, Lord Jesus, in the silence of our being. We pray for these people. Let nothing distract us, Jesus, in this moment of prayer.

Lord Jesus, straighten any legs that need to be healed and put all the connective tissues and the bones together that should be put together. Heal also our lungs from emphysema, from asthma. If any man, woman, or teen wants to be freed of addiction to cigarette smoking or drugs, Lord, just release him. We deliver them all right now from that. If anyone is addicted to alcohol, Lord Jesus, just release that person from it. In the name of Jesus Christ, let him or her be healed! We deliver these people, Lord Jesus, and we cast that spirit of intemperance out of them. And by Your most Sacred Heart, Lord, just renew and revitalize our own hearts.

Enter into that abdominal region of our being, Jesus, if there needs to be healing there. Lord, any men or women who have ulcers, ulcerative colitis, Lord Jesus, just let them be healed. Let it be soon. Lord, just let their worries be taken away from within.

If there are any ailments in the hands or the arms, Lord, enter into our hands and into our arms and heal them. Heal them right now. Just burn right through our bodies Jesus.

If there are any tumors or lumps in any parts of their bodies, Lord, let them be dissolved. Let them be dissolved by Your power and just let them pass out of the bodies. A purified body.

If there's any cancer, in the name of the Lord Jesus Christ, leukemia, we command that these growths and this sickness and disease of body and blood be totally healed, and to become new cells, that the old sick cells just cease to spread, and let them return to a normal rate of growth. O Lord, remove any cancerous growth. Replace and heal, Lord Jesus, with healthy tissue, healthy cells. We praise You, Jesus. We thank You, Jesus.

Lord, enter into the thighs and into the knees, into afflicted people's feet. Anyone suffering with spurs, Jesus, and ankle problems, just heal them. Heal anything that needs to be healed: bones, muscles, tissues, organs. Praise You, Jesus!

We pray for those who are older and just bent over with infirmities that come with age. Lord Jesus, just enter with Your peace and remove all the pain. Revitalize them, Jesus. Lord Jesus, heal Your people, bless Your people. O Jesus, if there is any barrier of any kind, O Lord, just break it right now.

Let us praise God right now, just praise Him. Praise and glorify Him. We praise You, Father, we glorify You! Blessed be Your holy name. Precious Jesus, loving Savior. All things are possible when we turn to God. For God has told us that "Greater is He who is in us, than he who is in the world." Jesus said, "I am come that they might have life and have it more abundantly!" Praise You, Jesus.   Amen.

For All Emotional or Physical Pain

Lord, we offer this prayer for those who are experiencing intense emotional or physical suffering. Lord, these are special deliverances that need to be executed to bring health to Your People. We ask You through this prayer to bless that person with arthritis, that person with asthma, that man or woman who suffers with bladder trouble, all those in agony because of bone fractures, the patients who suffer with cancer or leukemia, the persons who have cataracts of the eyes or cirrhosis of the liver, ear trouble, emphysema, eye trouble, headaches, heart disturbances, muscular and crippling diseases such as MS. And that man, that woman with high blood pressure, or any infection, Jesus, just bring Your healing power. And there are those suffering with influenza, kidney ailments, pneumonia, or stomach trouble, tumors of all sorts.

Go right now out there to that man or woman who is suffering with anxiety, and those suffering depression of all forms. Lord, just heal their anger with themselves and others or with situations, and, let them have deep self-contentment and know that You love them and value them. And to that man, woman, child, or teenager who's suffering with despondency or discouragement or doubt, Lord, bring Your hope. Heal that person who is addicted to any harmful substances, or to sex without love, rather than to love with sex and responsibility. Lord, bring healing to families that are in trouble, to alienated husbands and wives who are at the point of breaking. Their marriage is in trouble, Lord; please heal them.

There is so much pain in so many areas. Heal the person with sadness and emptiness and loneliness. Heal those who have sleepless nights, Lord Jesus. And heal those secret sorrows, Lord Jesus, and those tensions that bring pain. To the persons who struggle with unbelief, O Lord, be the object of their life, their hope, their faith, their love.

Heal us, Jesus, in our weakness and our worries. Lord Jesus, we have come before You. We ask that You bring Your healing power, the fullness of Your Holy Spirit. We ask this through the blood of Christ and in His Holy Name. Amen.

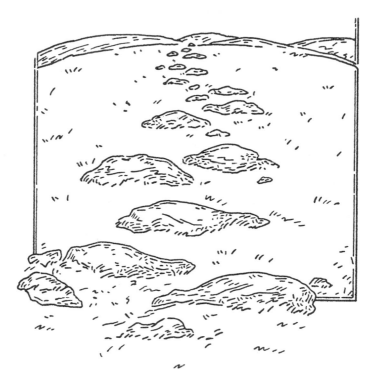

Use your broken humanity
as your stepping-stone to salvation.

Prayer of Deliverance from Visual Disturbances

Lord Jesus, unworthy as I am to be what You have called me to be, forgive me my weakness. Look at my heart of love and my desire to serve.

Lord Jesus, as in the days of the Apostles, confirm once again by signs and wonders your gift of healing. Give to those who suffer the bondage of blindness complete release from the ravaging diseases of darkness.

To you, foul infirmity of eye infection, disease, blindness, myopia, astigmatism, crossed eyes, conjunctivitis, and all eye irritations, you, Foul Spirit, I command you—in the name of Jesus, I adjure you—in the name of Jesus Christ, the Son of God, COME OUT OF THESE EYES! COME OUT AND NEVER RETURN!   Amen.

For the Hospitalized

Lord, we pray for the well-being of any person who is going into surgery this day or any day that the surgery will be in the hands of efficient ministers of medicine. Lord, we pray for all those in hospital, and those who care for them. We pray, too, for the comatose, the unconscious, and all who are to die this day. Bless them and heal them in desire and make them one with You.   Amen.

For Little Children

Lord, we pray for all the sick children. Especially, Jesus, those who have come forth with cerebral palsy or Down's Syndrome. Lord, we just ask You to make all things new again, Father, and help these children to unfold to be healthy, Jesus. All those in hospitals who are deformed with back problems or brain damage or hearing problems, the blind, the deaf, the crippled. Lord Jesus, just heal them today.   Amen.

A Community Prayer

Lord and Savior Jesus, we thank You for this opportunity in our lives for this very moment, Jesus, that You have allowed us to correspond with Your grace, Your call, Your love. We come here to be united with our brothers and sisters of all races and all different creeds or denominations, in the unity of Jesus Christ and in the unity of the Holy Spirit. Praise You, Father, for bringing Your family home, bringing us home.

Jesus, so many of us have walked so many different paths in life. Some of us, Lord, have found life to make promises that it didn't keep. Lord, we try to escape from ourselves and we try to escape from our obligations. So, Lord Jesus, we ask You to heal us right now and purify us and give us the inner spiritual life. And, Lord, we probably have forfeited that life by our behavior or our decisions many times. Lord, we receive the gift of birth but we have not lived that birth as we ought to, Lord Jesus. Some of us, Lord, as we grow older think that perhaps we were being prudent, by acting in certain ways. Lord, we might be domineering or the like.

Lord, perhaps some young girl or some older woman had a father who was extremely harsh and cruel to her. Perhaps, Lord, he has passed on and the peace was never restored between them. Perhaps there is a daughter, Jesus, who wanted to be closer to her father, or a son who wanted to be closer to his father. A son who tried to look to his father as a number one man in his own esteem. Perhaps a young man has seen his father as an alcoholic or a drunkard or perhaps beating up his wife or things of that sort. Those are wounds, Jesus, to be healed.

Others of us, Jesus, are to be grateful for good parents and responsible parents; but then, Lord, perhaps they were so good to us that we were not good to them. We hurt them, rejected them. What an awful thing to be rejected as a person. So, Jesus, go to our brothers and sisters whoever we may be and heal the wounds of rejection, Lord. Many of us have escaped to other parts or other areas of the world, thinking that perhaps in going away we would find new adventures, new experiences. Yet, Lord, we brought our own personalities with us, our own characters, our own traits, and the same problems just stayed with us.

Bind up our scars, Lord, and unite us again in Your peace and saving grace. We ask this through our Savior, Jesus. Amen.

For Miracles and Blessings

Lord Jesus, we ask You to look down upon Your people to-day, these people who have come from all over the country. Lord, we ask You to give them miracles, to give them the real gift of gifts, Yourself. Grant that asking for You, Jesus, they will receive God's blessings in its fullness. Let this be a peaceful day, a joyful day, a happy day, a day of health renewed in spirit, mind, and soul. We ask this through the power of the Holy Spirit and through the intercession of Mary, the Mother of God.   Amen.

The Living Christ

O Father, how human we are, how constantly broken we become, when we allow ourselves to direct ourselves. O Lord, just accept our surrender to You and, Lord, we ask You to take over our sicknesses and diseases and whatever might ail us.

Lord, we praise You and we thank You and glorify You for the gift of life. Lord, make supportive friendship a reality, a truth, a loyalty to You and commitment to one another. Jesus, speak to us of Your salvation, speak to us of Your salvation, Your healing, by speaking to us of You—You who were sent from the Father to save mankind from their mistakes, their errancies, and You, Jesus, who wanted to stay with us to the end of time by giving us Your Holy Spirit. Send that Spirit upon us, God, upon all your wonderful people. O God, they are the saints, not we; they are the saints because in their brokenness, their sinfulness, their mistakes, they do not deny it. They come forth and say *mea culpa,* through my fault. Lord, you have never forsaken or turned your ear away from the cry of a penitent sinner. Forgive me, God. Hear the cry of your penitent people. Go into their hearts now, Lord, and beat there with a new thrill. Let that faith just become alive; let that faith enkindle hope for a great expectation for a better tomorrow. And, Lord, raise us up to express our love to You by service of Love. We thank You, Jesus, and we praise You, Father.   Amen.

Prayers for Employment

Father in Heaven, I am a human being with the human rights You have endowed me with. Marriage has been a vehicle I have chosen as my way to salvation. You have entrusted me with a home, a wife, a child. I place into Your hands the welfare of this awesome responsibility, especially in this dire moment of need. Lord, I have no job! Lord, I am capable and most willing to delve into the vast arena of labor. Help me, Lord! It is Your will that each human person accepts the duty of work. In Your infinite kindness, in Your Divine Providence, lead me to that work which somewhere in this time You have prepared for me. I ask this request through the merits of Your sincerity in dying for me.   Amen.

Dear God, there must be a place for me in the vineyard of honest work. I have sought and sought, but the doors seem shut: "No place for you here."

Lord, I feel like a wanderer, a person without a compass, nevertheless forcibly bound to the needs of human existence. Lead, dear Lord, my wandering feet, my searching spirit, to that place of labor worthy of my human needs.

To Sustain One in Work

You have provided work for me, O Lord, and I thank You for that grace. Be with me, O Lord, as I undertake this day's work. Be at my side, O Lord, so that I may be faithful in the discharge of my assignments and my duties. Direct me, O Lord, to be honorable both to myself and in all my dealings with others. Lord, You know the weakness within me. Stay at my side that I may retain composure, self-control in speech and in temper. With Your perspective, may I go forth with Your purity. With the purity of Your perspective, grant me the power of Your Holy Spirit. In so doing, dear Lord, I will be able to live with myself, and be a radiant good example to others. Thus with the Christian spirit of humility and thoughtfulness, I will glorify You and edify others.

Before the Tabernacle

O my Lord Jesus Christ, the day has come. The day has gone. This day, O Lord, is spent. O Lord, all the days of my life are passing so rapidly and shall be returned to me in the agelessness of eternity. My years, O God, have accumulated, the night is near. Oh hide Thyself not from me. I steal tonight my self away into the silence and requiem of prayer before Your Holy Presence. Allow me, O Lord, tonight, to pray for the whole world, for the sick, the suffering. May Your presence come upon them. Lord, where there is doubt, allow me to bring Your faith. Where there is despair, Your hope. Where there is darkness, light. Where there is sadness, the joy of Your presence. O Master, allow me and my staff, allow all whom You call to ministry, to give to the world the love of Christ.   Amen.

Holy Hour

Lord Jesus, we gather here to give You consolation, to bring You worship and adoration. We come here, Lord, to spend an hour with You, giving You companionship and seeking mercy for the world and for our own souls. Bring us into a deeper understanding of Your Passion, of the Blood—the precious Blood You shed for us.

As we come closer to Your wounded Humanity, blessed by your Divinity, allow this precious Blood to fall upon each one of us and to heal us in the Blood of the Lamb. We ask this through the power of Your Holy Childhood, through the power of Your suffering and death, and through the power of Your glorious Resurrection.   Amen.

If you spend an hour with Jesus in silence and in prayer, you're going to be different. One of two things will happen: either you will give up Jesus or you will give up what doesn't lead you to Jesus.

A Priest's Prayer

Lord, You know there are so many of us in this world who have goodwill, good intentions, but, Lord, each one of us has been called to a distinctive vocation, a distinctive place. So, Jesus, we ask that You will accept all our past efforts as an expression of love for You. Lord, we do not seek to raise up a person or personage or a ministry. It is the Lord Jesus Christ whom we raise up and, Lord, may we never speak, act, or think in any way that is contrary to You.

Lord, there are people with spiritual burdens who need more faith and more hope and more love. Lord, there are those persons who have psychological disturbances and difficulties in interpersonal relationships. Some have been seriously hampered and hurt. We're all wounded, God. Lord Jesus, we ask you as Peter did: "To whom are we to turn?"

O Lord Jesus, we thank you for what You have done for us. Lord, I am Your Priest and I am unworthy of this gift; but, Jesus, You gave it to me and I will die for it. God, I accept that death. May Your name be praised and glorified, Jesus. Give us many healings and blessings, Father, in spirit, soul, and body. Hallelujah, Lord, hallelujah, hallelujah!

Hurting One, We Hurt All

Father in Heaven, Lord Jesus, O Holy Spirit! My heart just breaks as I think of the broken body of Christ out there, of so many people in need. To them please bring Your healing power.

Lord, we ask that you bless anyone with arthritis, anyone suffering from fractured or broken bones or limbs, and all those with muscular or crippling diseases such as MS. To them, Lord Jesus, with the power of Your Holy Spirit, bring Your power of healing.

Lord, that we may walk again—with You!   Amen.

A Doctor's Prayer

Dear God, I look about and I see the anguish and the pain of man. The depths of my soul cry out, "What can I do?" Dear God, my humanity craves to heal. But why have You moved my heart so? For some reason, unknown to me, You have chosen me from so many more capable than I to be a physician. Yes, I am bound to the dictates of medicine. I am an instrument of healing. Oh how I tremble as I ponder this awesome responsibility! It is Your work, O Lord, not mine. Without You I know I cannot succeed. Lord, You have placed in my human hands the bodies of the sick. Give me Your skill. Help me to have clear vision—Your vision! Fill my heart with authentic sympathy, kindness. Do help me to overcome every temporal weakness. Strengthen me with whatever may enable me to protect and preserve life. Lord, human life is precious to You. You have consigned it to the earth as a gift of Your infinite love; You have eternalized it. Lord, You are the Great Physician. Before You I humbly bow in adoration. Before You I plead the cause of my vocation. Lord, make me worthy!   Amen.

To "Abba"

O dear Lord, on the night of Your Last Supper You promised not to leave us orphans. And we know, God, that You have kept Your promise by being with us because You have loved us. You have chosen us too. But as You told those first men, those first followers, men and women and children, as You told us, You did promise to send Your Holy Spirit so that He would recall all things that You would proclaim.

So, dear God, on every man, woman, and child in this country and in all parts of the world, just continue to send forth that Spirit that we may know Your love, adore You, and proclaim You, and surrender to You, and thus receive Your healing mercy.

O Lord Jesus, we pray for the afflicted. We bring to You and to Your Heavenly Father all those who have asked that we should pray for them and we beseech You, God, though we do not know all their names, that You would know their names as You do, that You shall find them, bring them to the feet of love, bless them, and restore them. We pray, Father, for those who are looking into the faces of them, that nurse them and care for them. O Father, our "Abba," we love You, we praise You, and we glorify You. Bless them, Father. Amen.

When Falling Short

O Father, how truly weak we are. This is not exactly news to You. Every day, in many ways, our humanity breaks forth. We start out with marvelous intentions. We end up trying to get even, to get out of responsibility, to nurture dishonesty and thoughtlessness. O Lord, forgive us. Your Son knew us well. We know now what to do; even more, let us have some of Your power, so that we may forgive one another and be healed.   Amen.

For Psychological Problems

Father, we pray for those psychiatric patients who are disturbed right now with some form of psychosis, whether it's depression, schizophrenia, or paranoia. And, Lord Jesus, those who may be suffering with alcoholic psychosis. The damage has already been done to the cerebral nervous system. Lord, we pray for those who have this problem that is also affecting them in their brain cells. Jesus, we ask that You bring them the fullness of Your blessing. Bring Your Healing Power, Lord, as only You can do.

We pray for all who are sick with neuroses and dissipation, Lord, and other forms of phobia—all neurotics and psychotics, Lord. We ask you to go into their beings that they may recognize who they are and what they are, Lord Jesus, and give that being to You to be healed.

Lord, we pray too for those with personality problems or disorders, those who are antisocial because they themselves, Lord, are not accepting themselves. We pray for all these psychological disturbances and invoke Your Healing Love on all the afflicted.   Amen.

For Our Deep-Seated Hurts

Lord Jesus, allow us to resurrect consciously all that is in the quagmire deep inside us, in our subconscious. Lord Jesus, and even deeper than that. We're not going to be afraid. We're going to be able to take this pain and this guilt. It's good to have guilt, God, as long as we know there is One Who will take it away and not just cover it up.

Repair our egos, God. Lay Your hands on our deepest mental wounds, Lord, and bless them. We forgive all those in our past life who have hurt us. Whatever feelings and thoughts we have internalized, whatever mistakes—real or imagined—we have committed, we ask that You unloose right now. Free us of resentment, anger, regrets, bitterness, and a judgmental attitude.

Lord, You who make all things whole and new, we stand before You in faith, acknowledging our weaknesses and begging for Your strength and Your love which alone restore us to security and peace.   Amen.

God's hurt is people's broken brotherhood.

Healing Love

Lord, You have told us to ask and we will receive,
  to seek and we will find,
  to knock and You will open the door to us.
I trust in Your love for me
  and in the healing power of Your compassion.
I praise You and thank You for the mercy You have shown to me.
Lord, I am sorry for all my sins.
I ask for Your help in renouncing the sinful patterns of my life.
I accept with all my heart Your forgiving love.
And I ask for the grace to be aware
  of the disorders that exist within myself.
Let me not offend You by my weak human nature
  or by my impatience, resentment, or neglect
  of people who are a part of my life.
Rather, teach me the gift of understanding and
  the ability to forgive, just as You continue to forgive me.
I seek Your strength and Your peace so that I may become
  Your instrument in sharing those gifts with others.
Guide me in my prayer that I might know what needs to be
  healed and how to ask You for that healing.
It is You, Lord, Whom I seek.
Please enter the door of my heart
  and fill me with the presence of Your Spirit now and forever.
I thank you, Lord, for doing this.   Amen.

REFLECTIONS

Why are you calling me, Lord?
 "Because you are a sinner
 Because you are empty
 Because I know inside of you and you've got love
 Because I know you want perfection
 Because I know you'll give yourself to Me.
 You can be My Hands, My Eyes, and My Feet,
   My Heart, My Lips."

Fearful of Rejection

Why are you so frightened? That's a very important question to ask in your life. Why are you frightened? Jesus asked that question. Why do you doubt that it is really I, said Jesus. Perhaps that is why you frighten another or why you yourself are frightened. Listen to that word, frightened. Are you afraid to make yourself known, to reveal yourself? Are you afraid that perhaps by being disclosed, being known, you might be rejected?

Whatever difficulty you may be experiencing—perplexities, hardships, brokenness, family disturbances—remember, God is with you. You do not have to be frightened. You do not have to fear that you are going to be rejected. God hasn't rejected you, and God, though He was frightened to die as Man, went to the Cross to heal you, to enrich you. You are precious. Try to say this to yourself over and over again. Not just verbally pronouncing it, but convincing yourself. Say this —in fact, say it with me: "I must learn more of my own strengths and learn to like, yes, and to love myself. I must care enough about myself and about others."

That's why God died for you. That's why God was born. That is why God conquered death and gave us the Resurrection. He loves us, *just as we are.* So any fear or self-doubt that's in you, I cast out in the Power of the Anointing of Healing Spirit, of Healing Love. In the name of the Father, and of the Son, and of the Holy Spirit.   Amen.

You Are Important to God

You must understand something, that you are important to God. You are not a nobody, you are somebody. You are a person. Jesus died for you. Try to take yourself right now beneath the Cross of Jesus with your burden, your problem, your ache, your suffering. Look up to those wounds right now, and give your suffering to the Lord Jesus Christ. He was upon that Cross just for you, for me, for every man, woman, and child; and you are important. Jesus hears our voice, our cry.

I'm asking you right now to fall upon your knee, in your need. It is time for us to pray to the Lord. And remember, you are important, and healing is for you, no matter what the sickness is. You might have cancer, leukemia, a broken heart. You may have a heart condition, diabetes, blood disease, a broken home. You may be on the verge of a divorce. God wants to heal you. God loves you. God did not make those circumstances. We have brought those circumstances about, so now let's pray. Let's rebuke Satan and cast him out of our life, and pray in faith. Pray with me, won't you please?

O my Father in Heaven, Lord Jesus, Holy Spirit, I am sorry for all my sins, and I ask for Your help in renouncing sinfulness, and I renounce Satan. I accept You my Lord, Jesus Christ, as my Lord and Savior. Enter within my heart with Your Holy Spirit. Send Your precious blood upon me, and heal me. I cast this sickness out, and I believe it is leaving me, and I will act on the promises of Scripture, on the promises of Your life, for the good You have done. Receive me, Jesus. I seek Your strength, Your peace, that I may become Your instrument and witness the wonderful things You are doing for me.   Amen.

For Disorders

You are a child of God, and God has promises for you—yes, promises to heal you and make you well, and make you prosperous. Therefore at this moment, I want to take you right into Scripture, where a man who was lame had a new chance. As Peter passed through the temple gates, the Scriptures tell us that a layman begged Him for alms, and Peter said: "What I have, I will give you. In the name of Jesus Christ, rise and walk." That man rose, and that man entered the temple to praise God, and he walked into his world to witness that God is a miracle God. [Acts 3:1–8].

Right now, I ask that you kneel down and pray with me, and let me pray with you—not *for* one another, but *with* one another. We should pray: "Give us this day, O Lord, yes, give us this day." Did you know that life with God begins with a new clean slate, and all success with God begins truly with a clean chapter in the autobiography of your life. That brings success. It brings real fulfillment. It brings life, and God wants that for you. An old Evangelist once said: "If you want what God wants, and you want it for the reason God wants, then the Holy Spirit will be with you."

Let's pray together to God:

I ask for the grace to be aware of the disorders, dear God, that exist within myself. I take my own responsibility right now. Let me not offend You any more, my God, through my weak human nature. I bring You, dear God, my impatience, my neglect, my brokenness, my sickness, and I cast it out of me in the name of Jesus. I seek Your strength, Your peace, Your life. Let this prayer, dear God, bring healing to me right now.   Amen.

Jesus Calms the Storms

Healing is part of your Salvation. The promises of Scripture are not only for your soul, not only for your spiritual life, but also for your body. You have to act on those promises of Christ. We all have storms in life, don't we? That's a deep pain to human nature. Would you turn to Matthew 9, read it after you hear my prayer, meditate on it today, and let the healing love of Christ continue from this prayer, this anointed prayer.

There was a storm on the lake, and the Scriptures tell us Jesus got into the boat and His Disciples followed Him. Without warning, a violent storm came up on the lake, and the boat began to be swamped by the waves. Jesus was sleeping soundly, so they made their way toward Him and they woke Jesus up saying, "Lord, Lord, save us. *Domine, salva nos.* We are lost." He said to them, "Where is your courage? How little faith you have." Then He stood up. He took the winds and the sea to task, and complete calm ensued, and the men were confused. They were dumbfounded at the power of Him who was in their boat.

My dear friends in Christ, God wants to come into your life. You are important, very important. Don't you ever forget that. What a tragedy not to avail oneself of the power of Jesus. God sent Him with power to heal. God gave us Pentecost through Christ, and that is power. God is an uplifter.

He's not a downer. And God will take you right now to the top of the mountain. God will calm those storms in your life. Will you pray with me right now? Pray and believe.

O my God, I come to you. I bring my brokenness to you, my emptiness to you. Guide me in my prayer with this Priest who is praying with me, whose ministry staff also pray for me, that I might know what needs to be healed and how to ask You for that healing. Whatever makes me anxious or worried or fearful, in the power of the Gospel, in the power of this prayer, I cast out. I rebuke Satan. I rebuke this storm completely and I avail myself of the healing, calming Christ. I pray in the name of Jesus. I pray, I believe, and I will live.   Amen.

God Is Near

The Book of Exodus 17:7 says, "Is the Lord among us, or not?" Now that's a question many of us ask when we have trials. Haven't you asked that question sometimes? Is God really among us? Is He close to me? But to ask this question is really to tempt God. The great certainty of our life with God is the assurance that He is there working and leading in our lives always. Whether or not we see His hand or sense His presence, God is near us.

I want you to avail yourself in God's presence. God is calling you. God is calling you to enrich your life, on the promises of God. God says in Exodus 15:25, "I am the Lord that heals." God is giving Himself a name. He's calling Himself Healer, and God will forgive any mistakes that you have made, any sins.

Read Mark, read Luke, read Matthew, read John, read the Apostles. See what Peter did, what Paul did. They went with power and the power produced healings of all sorts, and then the people were confirmed in the preaching of Jesus.

It's my privilege to pray with you, and this prayer doesn't end here. I'm bringing this every day to my daily Mass, to my daily Holy Hour before the Blessed Sacrament, and my people do the same thing. My staff loves you. You are important to us. Remember this encouraging thought from Psalm 103:

"It is He who forgives all your guilt, who heals every one of your ills, who redeems your life from the grave, who crowns you with love and compassion, who fills your life with good things." I pray in that promise. I pray in the name of Jesus.

The answers to your life are in your heart, and that is Jesus. Discover the God that's already in you. You are important.

On Love

1 Corinthians 13:4 tells us, "Love suffers long, but love is kind." What is this kindness of love? It is this: that no matter how much love is ill-treated or scorned, how much it is ignored or neglected, how little return or requital is given to it, yet, love suffers all these things, it stays kind. It has a fixedness, if I may use that word. Love maintains firmness, concreteness, substance, amid all sorts of slights and lack of appreciation. It stays constant.

I frequently think about this, that when we love another person it's not necessary to have feelings. Feelings pass away, but the love can remain. Love means this: that I through my life give you an occasion, an opportunity, a circumstance, to make you grow to be what you were meant to be. When I see you be what you are, I find joy. Oh what a Grace that is for both of us. I want to pray for you right now, that if any discouragement comes into your life, any brokenness, you will give it to the Lord Jesus Christ. Look at that depression, go into that anger, and find the need for your self-contentment. God wants you well. God loves you, and in His holy name, I cast out all forms of sickness and disease of mind, spirit, and body. In the name of Jesus, my friend, be healed, be healed.   Amen.

God Is Our Strength

Through the years I've discovered there's something very special about two people either writing to each other or praying with each other. I've also seen, so often, that a close relationship can be developed, yes, a deeper relationship in Christ Jesus. I'd like to pray with you at this moment that you may have strength.

Isaiah 25:4 tells us, "Thou hast been a strength, a refuge, a shadow." What does this mean? In my thinking, there are times in life when we are distressed through illness, unemployment, accidents, and a host of many other things. In such times the Lord is a Strength. Though the storm of adversity blows, He is the Refuge. What of the heat of opposition, especially hurt and opposition that comes from those who should know better? The Lord is there, however, to be our shadow. Oh yes, in His presence, we can be happy. In His presence, we can be secure. In His presence, all our afflictions will go away. In His presence, we can conquer. In His presence, all our suffering will be healed.

God loves you! God is calling you. God wants to heal you! We need to go where the need is greatest. I come to you in prayer in the name of Jesus. Any weakening sickness or disease that you have, I rebuke. And I bless you right now, in the name of Christ our Savior, who is your Lord, your Master, your Healer.   Amen.

For Teenagers

No teacher, no Priest, no Minister, no politician, nobody has a right to say that you're not important. You're going to be tomorrow's doctors, lawyers, professors, teachers, husbands, wives. I want you to kneel down with me right now and thank God for life.

Lord Jesus, take these teenagers right now with hearts full of life and spirits that want to give themselves to You and to the whole world, doing good. Jesus, free these teenagers right now from any perplexity, doubt, hardship, addiction. Anything that's in them discouraging them, destroying them. Teach them that you are their Father, their Father in Heaven, and that Jesus is their Brother. Let them stand for good and cast out evil. Keep them pure and holy. Let them realize the power that they have in holiness, in union with You, which expresses itself in continency, in good thinking, in balance, and in health. Raise them up to the glory and dignity of good men and good women, Your children.   Amen.

On Aging

The Scriptures tell us, "Thou art old and stricken in years and there remaineth yet very much land to be possessed." [Josh. 13:1] That's encouraging.

We hesitate at times to tell people that they are getting old, but God has no such inhibitions. We need to be reminded that our days are numbered, yes, and we will die. We will use this life as a stepping-stone for the crown of eternal life in Heaven. However, we need to anticipate the day when we will no longer be able to function for the Lord by buying up the opportunity of today. Today is yours. Tomorrow, we're not sure. The past is gone. The night of life fast approaches when no man can work. Recall what Moses tried to write when he said, "So teach us to number our days, that we may apply our hearts unto wisdom."

My dear friend, you may have written to us, or you may have called us.

God is trying to tell you something. He's trying to tell you that you are born with destiny. You have a predestined hour. I am here as God's hour to tell you that you are important. God's message, as before, is alive now. God heals! He heals now for you, right now! If there is deafness, a heart condition, mental disturbances, arthritis, anything, God heals! He made a promise and He accepts your prayer.

I'm praying for you, whether sickness or disease is coming to you from old age, from wherever it comes, I take authority under God's authoritative power to bless you. Be healed in Jesus' name. I adjure sickness to leave you in the name of Jesus. My friend, please live and act on this prayer of faith. Amen.

For Shut-Ins: Life Is Not Over!

Did you know that your bed of pain, your wheelchair, your isolation, is your altar of sacrifice? Just because you may have advanced with the years of wisdom does not mean that life is over for you. In fact, life is never over, even when we close our eyes to the sensitivity of this world's existence. When we close our eyes to this world, we open up with the eyes of our immortal soul to the heaven beyond.

You have sickness. You have some ailment that has made you a prisoner—perhaps a prisoner in your own home—a victim on your altar of pain. But pain is not bearable when we look upon it as suffering alone. Pain is bearable when we look upon it as love, love for someone. A mother suffers her pain for her sick child. A father suffers a similar pain in an unpretentious manner, a humble way. He cannot verbalize the anguish of a sick son, a sick daughter, a sick wife, but he too suffers. What keeps him? What keeps a courageous mother going on? Love. And the price of love is sacrifice.

Your life is not wasted. Would you like to save a soul? Would you like to save a husband, a child, a friend, or a stranger who because of your loving pain and sacrifice can become a friend, a friend of Jesus, a friend of God, *your* friend? Won't you look upon your pain as an opportunity for redemptive suffering. You can get rid of that pain if you wish by cursing it.

But if you are one of those victim souls whom God is

inviting to share the suffering on His Cross, then God can come into the evil of your pain and your suffering, cleanse it, and make it an occasion for health. He can make it an occasion for meritorious opportunities to do good.

Whatever that pain might be, let us pray:

Lord Jesus, we have become victims of suffering and pain, but we want to be victims of love and take that pain and transform it into a stepping-stone for health, success, both for ourselves and for others. You, foul sickness of disease, we curse you not as evil in itself, because you are not evil in yourself, but you have evil by its cause, Satan. We cast you out of this sickness, this disease, and we will use this pain, this anguish, as a means, an occasion, to do good. Heavenly Father, receive my life, receive my body, my spirit, my soul. Make me a channel of Your Grace of healing for myself and for others.   Amen.

Brokenness

Only God can make new that which is broken. Are you broken? At times, I'm broken. We all are. Your family members experience brokenness. But did you know that in brokenness we can recognize how frail and fragile we are. Look at your brokenness; and whatever the cause is, do not try to disturb yourself with that but think of the One who can make new that which is broken.

Are you suffering depression? Are you suffering any type of physical disturbance, mental anguish, economic hardship? Other problems or difficulties? If you are married, is there a break in your relationship, a rejection in your marriage? Are you on the voyage of a wreck, instead of on a voyage of discovery? If you want to know who you are, where you are going, it is time to fall upon your knees and look up. If you know who your God is, everything will fall into its proper place, like the parts of a jigsaw puzzle—disjointed pieces being put together and making a beautiful whole. That's beautiful you! You're God's child, and God created you for Himself. Won't you turn to Him right now?

Pray with me:

> Lord Jesus Christ, You are the Son of God, and I have faith that You are truly a living God, not a dead God. We live in the Resurrection Power. Lord, baptize me afresh with the gift of Your Pentecostal Spirit. Send Your Holy

Spirit. Renew me, bless me, inside, outside, all of me, completely. I give myself to You completely, Lord Jesus. I will come to You, Jesus, and I care enough about You, Jesus, to allow You to care enough about me and to heal me. I take authority right now over any ailment, any psychological disturbance, any emotional upset, anything that is bothering me, that keeps me in brokenness. I will rise from my brokenness and see the Glory of Your hand healing me. You, foul sickness, disease, come out of me, in the name of Jesus! I trust in faith. I trust in this prayer. Lord Jesus, I am Yours.   Amen.

Peace

Giving thanks to God is a secret to sustaining peace. Yet every year somewhere between two and three hundred thousand Americans give up seeking peace, and they attempt to commit suicide. Did you know that on Christmas Eve in New York City the suicide hotline receives one call every minute from people who feel that they cannot face life any longer?

Not all of the people who are struggling in this way are unsaved. God's people, that is what He wants you to know, are important to Him. So if you say, "I don't have peace," I want you to look at the Lord Jesus Christ right now. Jesus was sent to us by the Father to bring us the peace. If you give your weaknesses to God, they can be purified and they can become strength. Think of the Christmas Story, the story of a birth. God wants to be born in your life. He wants to give birth to your strengths which are now camouflaged by your weaknesses. The night before He was crucified Jesus said, "Peace, peace I leave with you. My peace I give to you. As the world gives it, I do not give it in that fashion, I give you My peace."

Lord Jesus, if any one needs help right now, I'm turning to You, as Your consecrated servant, Your Priest, and I ask You to bless this person and give this wonderful person the peace and joy that come from Your birth.

Be peaceful in Jesus' Holy Name.   Amen.

Trust in God

My dear friend, thank God with me, first for your life, then for the circumstances that encircle your life, even the hard ones. You can take those hard circumstances and you can change them into a new birth of strength that leads to virtue. You know, all of us want to be able to enjoy and to have God's peace even in the most painful experiences of life. Please pray with me right now and pray from your heart. We don't need a prayer book. All we need is the prayer book of our hearts. When we pray with God, we pray exactly with what's inside of us. We cry, we laugh, we smile. We tell him exactly what's disturbing us, and there's a peace that comes to us. I will be able to thank God in every difficulty when I understand God's ultimate objective in allowing that difficulty in my life, some people say. But you know, you can thank God with me for all the circumstances He has allowed to take place to purify you and me and cleanse us. Let's give thanks to God, in everything, give thanks. That's what St. Paul tells us and His peace of healing will come into your life and protect you from torments, bitterness, and the memories of the past. May almighty God bless you, the Father, the Son, and the Holy Spirit.   Amen.

If we love love,
if we love friendliness,
if we love helpfulness,
if we love beauty,
if we love health,
if we love to create joy,
if we love usefulness,
and are not self-seekers,
the Spirit, which expresses itself in love,
and helpfulness, and beauty,
will enter into us,
and abide there.
Oh yes, then we become what we love.

For a Troubled Marriage

Perhaps some misunderstanding has come between you and your marriage partner. Perhaps you'd like to get even and retaliate. Perhaps you're entertaining the thought of a divorce. Divorce is not the answer. You've got to go back to the roots, the roots of love, to keep your marriage together. You've got to go back with humility.

Christian marriage is probably the most romantic story on earth. There's no question about that, but you did not marry romance. You married a person, and each one of you is important. You're a child of God, and whoever mocks love, outrages human nature. Those who embrace love within the context of Christian living will find happiness and fulfillment because they place their source in God.

I'd like to pray with you right now. Your marriage is important to you, to your partner, and to your children, if God has given you a family. It's important to society, important to the Church, because it's important to God. Won't you with humility right now, just kneel down where you are, in your living room, your kitchen, your bedroom. Close your eyes right now and open your heart. Just picture God coming into your room right now and saying to you in the voice of your partner, your husband, your wife, "I love you, I love you, I love you, and I renew my love before God with you."

As a minister of God, I pray for you that you may be moved and touched, as may your spouse, to save your marriage. In the name of Jesus, may this marriage be blessed, and all evil disappear.   Amen.

Reconsecrating Marriage

I'd like to speak in the name of Jesus right now, who says to you and your partner: "I love you, I called you from the very beginning to be one, and I don't want your personalities to clash to such a point that you're going to destroy what I made for you. You are important, each one of you, and I need you to build My creation. Long before there was earth, or the sun or the stars ever existed, there was God, my Father. He's the Creator of all life, and you're part of that life."

He is the cause of all that is good, and in His own time, and according to His own plan and wisdom, God made the Heavens and the Earth. All the things were made by Him, and through everything that was made God was expressing Himself in His great love. The Bible tells us it was good. Our teachings of the Holy Word tell us that everything God made was good. From that first moment of darkness, out of nothing, God created Adam and Eve, and from those two lovers, who made a mistake, hardship came into the world.

Sometimes marriages seem to be going on the rocks. You know what causes marriages to break? Selfishness. We know difficulties will come, and come with a purpose. We must try to find that purpose. Perhaps it is a need to rediscover each other, that God still wants to be born in each one of you.

O Father in Heaven, I pray for this wonderful couple, each partner, and I dedicate them back to You. Let them renew their vows, right now, before You, God.

O Father in Heaven, consecrate their life, their love completely, to Your worship and to the building up of humanity. Anything that is trying to destroy your marriage, I take authority over it right now, in the mighty name of Jesus. In the mighty name of Jesus, I cast it out of your pathway, out of your life.

O Father in Heaven, let my words be heard right now, received, assimilated, and fulfilled. God, you appointed each one of us to serve You, so that one day we could come and stand before You in the fullness of life and love. Amen.

Affirming Your Spouse

Perhaps you have sought to discover the world and what it offers, and that has proven to have been your first mistake. As you looked distractedly at what the world could offer you, what you could obtain from the world, you forgot that the real journey of discovery was learning who *she* is, who *he* is. That's the joy of marriage. You are married not to a body, not to a soul. You are bound together in God's grace and love and life to a *person;* and that person, as time passes, as the years go on, needs to be *affirmed*—as a person—by your person.

You are important to each other. Hardships come. Difficulties are attacking you. Perhaps your spouse has become an alcoholic because the responsibilities of life and work are overburdening. He or she seeks an escape. You can restore your spouse. Perhaps your children are raised and gone and now the house is an empty shell, no longer a home with the noise and bustle and the chattering of children. This is often a problem—as, for example, the mother feeling left aside, taken for granted, forgotten, unappreciated. She needs to be affirmed.

God is giving you a new phase in your marriage. Together, you can ride these problems and make this voyage of discovery of self. I would hope that you each turn to your spouse and with real humility say to each other: I love you, I affirm you, I forgive. Please forgive the times that I have not affirmed you. Take my hand again. Take my heart with unconditional love to God that resurrects our love for each other. Let's say to each other: I must learn more of my own strengths and learn to like and to love myself. I must listen actively to you, and so listening I can discover your wants, your needs, your problems, and you will know my problems, my needs, my wants. I must care enough about you to look for and find your strengths, and I will consider it a privilege to provide positive reinforcement in you and build on your strengths. I will continue to stretch and to discover who and what I really can be by learning what you can truly be before God and me. Together we will expect the best. Yes, we don't have to expect perfection, but we can expect excellence from us, ourselves, as a gift to each other.

Lord Jesus, bless this couple. Whatever their problem is, it's very important and precious to them. Let them not turn their backs on each other by retaliating, especially by seeking divorce. But let both partners know that they are given to each other as a gift to eternity.   Amen.

For a Mother and Her Sick Child

You are a mother. You have a child. How beautiful you are with God creating life in your body. You have experienced the joy of movement within that temple of your flesh. God did not abandon you. You brought forth another human being. You've cuddled that human infant in your hands, your arms, you've nursed it, kissed it, you have embraced it, you see it grow.

But suddenly, unexpectedly, like an unforeseen stranger or a thief, sickness and disease comes into your home. It strikes almost deadly. Your child is ill. Tears come from your heart. Yes, more than tears from the eyes. You would almost die for that child. Only God knows that pain. Also his Mother knew that pain. And whether we are Catholic or Protestant or Jewish, God knows what pain is. He experienced that pain in His Son, Jesus. And because Jesus is alive and was Human, He had a Mother. She too knows what pain and anguish is.

I'd like to take you right now to your God who has not caused that sickness, that disease, but who wants to suffer in the fullness of His atonement, and He has suffered it for you and can help you rise with your child to new life. To whom are you to turn? You've done the best you could with the medical profession which has helped you so well. You've turned to friends and prayer comes in, your prayer groups and others supporting you. But have you approached God?

Let us kneel and pray:

Lord Jesus, words fail us when a mother must cry and ache for the life of her child. Lord, she's just a mother. To whom shall she turn but to You who have come to her side in her body when she conceived. O Jesus, You are our Brother, our Savior, our Lord, You are the Divine Healer. Come to this mother, come to her husband, come to the father of this child. Come and lay Your hands upon this little infant, upon this son growing, this daughter growing, upon this sick child who is so precious to You. Come with Your healing spirit. And you, foul sickness and disease, whether you are mental, physical, or spiritual, you have no authority over this child. This child belongs to God. We baptize it afresh, right now, in a fresh Baptism of the Holy Spirit, and we cast this ailment out in the Blood and the name of Jesus, in the power of the Word.   Amen.

Hearts in Desperation

Who can understand God's love? And yet we know God loves us! I think that's what you and I are looking for. God doesn't even love us, according to St. Thomas, because we're His children, He loves us because His trait is to love. And you're important to Him. And your need, my need, the needs of people around the world, are so apparent.

Just look around. Look at your family members. Why are they in pain? Why are you in pain? All we have to do is read a newspaper or watch the evening news. We listen to our friends and we listen to our family members as they share their hurts, their sorrows, their questions. Yet, you will be deeply touched by the lost, the helpless, the hopeless people existing in all the parts of the world, if you too can just cast your eyes, your heart upon the world that is not your own.

Try to plant a seed of love, a seed of concern in another person, and you will see that God cannot forget your concern for His broken body, and He will be your source, your strength. He will come back to you and bless you in the very needs that you cry for.

Sometimes when we're in pain and anguish, we proclaim, "Suddenly I am all alone as I make this journey, the journey of my life." And yet, no matter where we turn or how we turn, we must walk our path. And the only thought we must remember is "I have a goal." A goal to serve my God, serve others the best way I can, and in so serving God and others I too will have God's blessings upon me. In life we can continue to say, "I cannot change things. I can change only myself." I'm so glad that you have given me this chance to pray for your pain. Your pain is important.

If I can touch you, I know you'll touch another and your pain won't be in vain.

The Scriptures say, "When I sit in darkness, the Lord shall be light to me." [MIC. 7:8] I think what he's saying is this: calamities cannot destroy true confidence. And the darkness cannot delay the dawn. No, darkness must pass into dawn. God is light! He's not darkness. And you and myself may be in the dark sometimes today, at this moment, through pain, suffering, anguish, dissipation, despondency, rejection. And you and I can see no light upon our lives.

But prayer is like lightning. It strikes sharp and it brings the whole picture into focus. Prayer seems hard at times and there is no sense of even the Divine Presence, but be sure of this: the trial will not last one moment longer than God's purpose allows. See, God is purifying us, cleansing us. We're becoming Saints. Look into your situation right now and say, "Why is this situation this way?" You have an answer, and you find peace and joy, when you turn to God.

Won't you pray with me now? Give me this chance to pray with you. We're touching one another. Love is going through to you from God, through me. Feel the warmth of His love. Feel Christ enter into you with a new fresh Baptism of the Holy Spirit.

Lord Jesus, we turn to You in this moment of despondency, discouragement, hardship, sadness, whatever it might be, and we look at Your eyes that are pierced, pierced, Lord Jesus, Your skin that's pierced, Your mouth that's bleeding, Your hair shriveled right there with drying blood, the thorns there, and we take strength from Your passion. Bless this wonderful person, Jesus. Let the bells of Your Easter Sunday sing and sound and ring for us, that we can be alive. Yes, may God bless you at this moment, and I bless you from all sickness and disease, you, your family, your loved ones, in the name of Jesus, be totally blessed. Amen.

Surrender to God

You have trust and faith in the person of Jesus Christ. What does that mean? It means that you believe that God the Father, who created you, loves you so much that He allowed Himself to come to you in Jesus Christ, His Son. Jesus loves you. When Jesus came to this earth on that first Christmas night, God was offering hope for the times of deep personal problems and for discouragements. God was offering medicine, a Divine medicine for the pain and the suffering that death brings into people's lives, and for the world crises that bring uncertainty and fear to the hearts of many people. The hope that God offers goes beyond mere expectation and desire, and there is a new compact, a new agreement, through Jesus Christ. Yes, and this is done through Jesus who gives us His Holy Spirit, and that Holy Spirit abides in us, and it's an essential characteristic of every Christian. St. Paul tells us about trust, confidence, refuge in God, and the God of hope. [1 Cor. 13:8 and 13] I want you to memorize and make very personal your thinking about God's promises and provisions for you, that God has given us Christian hope.

Imagine if there were no God. What a despair we who walk this valley of tears, would be in. Psalm 42:11 says: "Why are you cast down, my soul? And why are you so disquieted within me? Hope, you and God, for I shall yet praise Him, who is the health of my countenance and my God!" And 2 Kings 10:15 says, "In your heart, let there be right, as my heart is with you, right." There are many translations to this concept. Another says this, "Is thy heart right as my heart is right with your heart?" Two hearts becoming one, palpitating. That's what God wants to do with you.

Perhaps you have not been really looking at life with God's eyes, with God's mind. Perhaps you have not been touching a person, a friend, or something with God. Suppose the Lord were to ask you or me about this right now. What would you say? What would I say? The condition of my heart is very important to Him. Thus, He instructs, "Keep your heart with all diligence." If I spend my day striving for wealth, ease, or popularity in a world where Christ had none, the result would be a heart that is set on things of the earth.

Jesus is saying to you, "I love you. Don't worry about your mistakes, your sins. Don't worry about those persons who ridiculed you. Just remember, I think highly of you. I died for you. Give me your hand. Give me your heart. I have new chapters in your life. Just step out in the waters, so to speak, as Peter did. Trust me, have confidence in me. I love you. I will give you everything back. I will not take those things from you that you think I am asking from you to deprive you. Of course not. I don't need those things, but they need Me, and you need Me, for existence. Just give Me yourself, and when you take Me, I'll give you the whole world back with Me, and that's the difference."

May Jesus bless you, and Mary, the Mother of Jesus, protect you; may all the Angels and the Saints hover over your home, your family, your loved ones. May nothing touch you, no evil. I command the evil spirits that seek to destroy men to leave you! You are God's property, you're precious, and may Almighty God bless you, the Father, the Son, and the Holy Spirit.   Amen.

Conversion: Jesus Is Calling You

Have you ever experienced a conversion? A conversion is a change from one point of view to another. A true conversion is one that has inner interests in a motivation, inner conviction that the opposite is better.

Many conversions reach their highest peak after one has touched the bottom. Perhaps that is why God speaks to us about the great power of humility, brokenness, conversion. The spiritual conversion is going away from brokenness, weakness, sin, whatever you wish to call it, anything that separates you from the purpose of your existence, God. God is our beginning. God is our end. The difficulty of reaching the end from our beginning is that at times we become perplexed, overwhelmed, engulfed by the waves that overpower us. We try to swim against the current.

God is knocking on your door. He knocks because He loves you, but He is knocking only on a door that has no latch on the outside. That door can be opened only from within, with your power to let the Guest in. God loves you. God cares for you. Will you admit Him? Give Him yourself. God is calling to you; hear His voice.

Have mercy on me, O Lord. *Kyrie Eleison*, Lord, have mercy. *Christe Eleison*, Christ have mercy. Forgive us, Lord.

And Saul, still breathing murderous threats against the Lord's Disciples, went to the High Priest and asked him for letters to the synagogues in Damascus, which would empower him to arrest and bring to Jerusalem anyone he might find, man or woman, living according to the way. As he traveled along that particular path to Damascus, approaching that city, a light from the sky suddenly flashed about him. He fell to the ground. At the same time he heard a voice saying, "Saul, Saul, why do you persecute me?" "Who are you, sir?" he asked. The voice answered, "I am Jesus, the one you are persecuting, but now get up and go into the city where you will be told what to do." And so Paul received his conversion, and he went there for a few days in blindness. But his heart, his mind, his spirit, began to see what he never saw before, that he was a child of God, called to a destiny: the destiny of the salvation of his own soul and the souls of others. The love he had for God must be expressed to others! He became the great apostle of the Gentiles.

God is calling you, too. God has many things to do with your life. Accept this message of conversion, for the Lord loves you. Will you hear Him? Will you give Him yourself or will you give Him, as did His persecutors on Calvary's heights, just vinegar and gall?

You know that you belong to God, and God loves you just because you are you. That's a trait of God. God uses many vehicles to touch the hearts of His people to remind them that He loves them. His arms are always outstretched. His hands always open. His heart always exposed. His eyes always searching. His smile always compassionate. His entire being always waiting. Yet we don't always recognize Him. When the risen Jesus appeared to Mary Magdalene, she did not know it was He. [John 20:14] "When Jesus appeared to His Apostles, they thought it was a ghost." [Luke 24:37] "When He appeared on the seashore, the Disciples did not know Him." [John 21:4]

Jesus has appeared to you. He appears to you through flowers, through nature, through a sunset, the rising of the sun, through another person's handclasp, another person's care. God uses another human being. Pray with me:

Father, I abandon myself into Your hands. Do with me as You will, for whatever You do, I thank You. I am ready for all, and I accept You. Forgive me, Lord Jesus, for my sins. Lord Jesus, come to me. Appear to me. Give me the religious experience of Your presence.

I bless you in the name of Jesus, in the name of the Father, and of the Son, and of the Holy Spirit.   Amen.

Go forth and change the world and don't be changed by it. God is at your side. Better still, God is in your heart, your life, your mind. Go and change the world for a better place in which to live.

Power of the Cross

We all think we have an answer for the world's problems. But that precisely *is* the problem: we're looking to men, to women, to things, to governments, as the source of strength. That's not where life comes from. Life comes from God, and God showed us how much He loved us by sending His Son on the Cross. God's the solution to your problems, our problems. Look to God as the Source right now. Step out in faith.

Let Him be your Father. All thought of self, let it just disappear. Turn to the Lord. Let go right now from your self-sufficiency, the idea that you can accomplish anything and everything. Without God's life, you and I can do nothing. So let's turn to the Lord right now. Be refreshed, renewed. Remember the value of the Blood of Jesus, the riches of Jesus on that Cross, which bring you grace, life, strength, and healing.

Let Jesus embrace you as you embrace Him. Let Him touch you with His wounded hands. For as Isaiah says to us, "By His stripes and by His wounds, we are healed." Yes, you are healed, in the name of the Father, and of the Son, and of the Holy Spirit.   Amen.

The Resurrection and You

Jesus is not dead. Jesus is alive! The tomb is empty. And because Jesus is not dead, because He's alive, because the tomb is empty, you can be blessed right now.

I'm touching you, right now, in the name of Jesus. I'm loving you as a visible sign, in the name of Jesus. I want you to find the strength from the thoughts that I want to share with you, and I make my prayer for you, that God's Graces be upon you. Every sickness and disease, leave you. May you have no spirit of infirmity. May health and prosperity in life be totally yours, because that belongs to you as a child of God, but above all, because God loves you. All this can come to you if you place your trust, your confidence, your faith, in the truth that Jesus is alive!

There was a Resurrection after the Crucifixion, and may that thought enrich your faith, and may you feel the living power of Christ working through you. Just listen to what Jesus wants you to reflect upon. He's alive! I pray in hope that the messages that God gave me, and I pass on to you, under inspiration/anointing, may enrich your life to come closer to the Lord Jesus Christ. St. John tells us, "Bear much fruit, and so prove to be my Disciples."

Your entire way of life is a living testimony that Christ is not dead, but that Christ is alive in you. God raised Him to life and allowed Him to be seen, not by the whole people, but by only certain witnesses whom He had chosen beforehand in Himself. And now we are those witnesses. We have eaten, we have drunk with Him, after His Resurrection. That tomb is empty, and He has ordered us to proclaim this to His people and to tell them that God has appointed Him to judge everyone, alive or dead.

Together, we may both wonder why God's plan is the way it is. We may even wonder why we are the ones He has chosen, but our inability to fathom the mind of God should not keep us from crying out and from not carrying out His instruction to us: "You shall be my witnesses until the end of time." Let us pray:

O Lord, help me. Help me to develop the fruit of love, especially in times of pressure. Father, You deserve honesty from the heart. Help me to walk honestly before You as a living witness to You. I will bear fruit, Lord Jesus, and I will prove to the world that I am Your Disciple. Amen.

CONCLUSION: SPEAK LORD, YOUR SERVANT LISTENS

"Come into My Heart," says the Lord,
"and I will give you a new heart."

Jesus Speaks to Us

Open your heart to Me. My son, My daughter, I need you for Myself. I have purposes for your life, purposes far beyond your present comprehension. Yes, I have truths concerning Myself to give to you, truths deeper and richer and more wonderful than your understanding has thus far taken in.

My son, My daughter, My child, open your heart. Open your heart wide to Me. I will fill you with my Holy Spirit and in so doing will satisfy the deepest longing of your soul.

Since time began, I revealed Myself to you. I came to you as a little child. I walked among you, did good for you. I blessed your little children, blessed the sick, the suffering, made the blind to see and the deaf to hear, the lame to walk. I went to the Cross for you. Never forget that. Do not be dismayed if you see Me hanging still on the Cross and being tortured through time and space by centuries of evil.

I will conquer. There will be a resurrection and I will come back and I will appear. I have called you into a deeper and deeper understanding of this, My love for you. Do not try to achieve on your own what only I can do. For I am your God. I am your Lord. In me, there is all truth. Just come to Me. Seek this truth. Seek Me in the world without first looking at anything or anyone else. You are Mine.

Come and look upon My cross, the cross of your salvation. Come to Me with your love and I will give you Mine. Behold

I am your Savior. Cast your gaze upon Me, for in Me you will find life. You will find a rainbow that leaps with hope for a better tomorrow. And it can be yours. With all your love, come to Me!